In

It a..... .... guas of war

—The author

GOD SHARED
MY FOXHOLES

The Authorized Memoirs of a World
War II Combat Marine on Bougainville,
Guam, and Iwo Jima

Pfc. JOSEPH FRIEDMAN, RETIRED

iUniverse, Inc.
New York   Bloomington

God Shared My Foxholes
The Authorized Memoirs of a World War II Combat
Marine on Bougainville, Guam, and Iwo Jima

iUniverse books may be ordered through booksellers or by contacting:

iUniverse
1663 Liberty Drive
Bloomington, IN 47403
www.iuniverse.com
1-800-Authors (1-800-288-4677)

Because of the dynamic nature of the Internet, any Web addresses or links contained in this book may have changed since publication and may no longer be valid. The views expressed in this work are solely those of the author and do not necessarily reflect the views of the publisher, and the publisher hereby disclaims any responsibility for them.

ISBN: 978-1-4502-3262-3 (pbk)
ISBN: 978-1-4502-3264-7 (cloth)
ISBN: 978-1-4502-3263-0 (ebook)

Printed in the United States of America

iUniverse rev. date: 5/28/10

DEDICATION

From a perspective of over a half-century of hindsight, I hope the narratives in this book will reveal that ultimately nothing is inscrutable. Reflecting on my memories has helped me gain insights that I share now with you, the reader, as truths. As a lasting final tribute to all my former comrades-in-arms, I am dedicating this book to their revered memory as an enduring legacy and an acknowledgement of their indomitable courage and incredible sacrifices.

CONTENTS

Introduction

Having read the myriad of books and magazine articles on World War II about the war's many military and political complexities, I never even thought about attempting to write an autobiography of my own personal wartime experiences while serving with the Twenty-First Regimental Combat Team, Third Marine Division. During a weekend at my home in Florida, my cousin, a contemporary of mine, seemed positively in awe at the many personal incidents, some seemingly funny and others somewhat tragic, that took place during my military service. What was so surprising to him was my apparent ability to remember and relate in detail so many verbatim accounts of action skirmishes I had engaged in during my twenty-seven months in the Pacific, of which six and one-half months were in actual combat.

In retrospect, I found it impossible to remember every detail over a twenty-seven-month ordeal, but by explaining the many incidents I experienced and could remember, I was surprised at how easily the narratives flowed. By attempting to write these experiences chronologically, I received mental flashbacks as each experience unfolded, along with the verbatim dialogue my memory would still allow me to recall. Although I could easily understand just what took place in one soldier's heart and mind in all of those individual and varied crises faced and endured during so many weeks and sometimes months in action, with some of the most drastic mental and physical privations imaginable, it was extremely difficult to record.

Very often over the past sixty years, there were times, especially during the night, when my thoughts harkened back to the war. My mind was consumed as to why and how I had survived so many close calls, when dozens of our young comrades around me perished. Often I would suddenly bolt up from bed in a cold sweat and commence pacing the floor, trying to rationalize that maybe I really did not survive the artillery and mortar explosions detonating so close to me that the orange flash and heat would stun me. Perhaps I have lived another life. For whatever reason, I could not find closure for these experiences. I feel a strong obligation to keep the memory of my dead comrades alive. How to finally interpret these reflections remains a constant mystery to me. How I will ever find closure, God only knows! I still trust that one of the great truisms is that time often heals, and hopefully all the tormenting memories will ultimately fade into oblivion.

When asked by friends and family over the post war years to give a personal interpretation of what emotions the foot soldier experiences in close combat, the answers are very complex. Most men, however, who have experienced frontline duty will tell you how absolutely imperative it is that each man stay alert and focused on what is taking place around him when engaged during a firefight. Fear in battle is a natural reaction, but to become immobilized by fear can often result in serious casualties. So often, those images of men frozen by fear have remained indelibly imprinted on my mind.

Battle-hardened soldiers engaged in close combat know how to react and assess a given situation without permitting their emotions to distract them from making intelligent judgments in the confusion and the anxiety that often take place during battle. The adrenaline charge one gets under battle conditions has the capacity to enable an individual soldier to achieve almost any physical feat. The personal effect of being victorious in battle is positively exhilarating, always acting as an enormous morale and confidence builder. As each soldier plays out his own part within his unit, what usually sustains him is the comradeship, duty, and loyalty to his brothers-in-arms. These are the most powerful of human emotions, which effectively solidify his unit as a unified, effective fighting force.

The Moment of Heroes

The accidental hero in combat often occurs as an irrational impulse. Some soldiers may not measure nor contemplate the consequences of their single-handed attempt to destroy the enemy's heavily defended emplacement.

Unfortunately, in most instances, a lone action of this type proves unsuccessful, and the loss of life regrettably results. Nonetheless, who is to say that by this singular action, this soldier should not be considered a hero?

But there is another more realistic approach to this identical scenario. While fully comprehending the enormous risk of singularly attacking the enemy's strongpoint, the soldier should, in consultation with his men, plan a more feasible way of eliminating the enemy's strongpoint with careful planning, and then destroy the intended target with no loss of life. By knowing full well in advance how dangerous the mission is and the risk it entails, by fully realizing the imminent danger beforehand and still attacking the enemy without hesitation, these men are in my opinion the ultimate heroes.

Marine line units during World War II were fortunate in not having to concern themselves with today's so-called rules of engagement. Our solemn duty was to destroy the enemy by force of arms, unconstrained by pseudo regulations when attacking the enemy's strongpoints at each center of gravity. Our marine frontline units managed to stay defiant in the face of adversity, yet remained humble in victory.

While trying to avoid pomposity and cautious of muddying the waters, this book's verbiage has tried to be uncomplicated in its descriptive combat narratives. Lest the names of America's fighting men fade into oblivion, may their heroic deeds reverberate in the heavens … forever.

Above and Beyond

Let us return in time a bit,
The year was forty-three;
The Marine Corps' Second Division
Would be making history.

This island called Tarawa,
The enemy felt secure,
"Our island is impregnable," they cried,
We answered, "yeah, no more!"

Three days and nights we battled,
All those lives we had to pay;
Never once did they back off,
Mass heroics claimed each day.

No doubt we fought more battles,
And Marines can cite their names;
In the jungles of Pacific Isles,
We earned our claim to fame.
—The author

Admittedly, after more than sixty years, my thoughts still harken back to those momentous years in the service of my country in World War II. As brutal as those many action skirmishes were, the intensity and excitement always aroused the deepest personal camaraderie in our fighting men.

We knew full well that the battles we engaged in were history-making events, which would probably never be equaled for sheer drama in our lifetimes. Some days my memory still gets jogged from low-flying aircraft or some distant summertime thunder. Even an offhand remark by someone in a golf foursome can precipitate a memory of past battle incidents; I am sometimes asked by fellow golf members why it seems at times that I'm so distant.

Every event described in this book is factual, and all those marines who are written about are actual persons. Some of the dates may not be precise, due to the lack of a calendar in foxholes. Considering that all events described are strictly from memory, any inaccuracy is not intentional, but rather due to the lapse of time since their occurrences more than sixty years ago.

At the time of Pearl Harbor, I was living on a small farm in Flemington, New Jersey. My father worked in New York City, and during the time he was away, I handled the many chores on our property to maintain it properly. The quiet evenings were usually spent discussing the war and listening to the radio, along with discussions about national and international affairs. My dad's perceptive analysis was amazing, and I gained a wide in-depth understanding of global affairs. When I enlisted in the Marine Corps in September 1942, I felt I had a fair understanding of the political ramifications that caused this war.

In the post-war era, I often tried to evaluate what physical and psychological factors of our World War II soldiers, sailors, and airmen made them so tenacious against such formidable enemies in some of the most sanguinary battles in the history of warfare. For America's fighting men, nothing was more sacred than avenging Pearl Harbor and the brutal death march of our army at Bataan by the Japanese in the latter stages of the Philippine Islands campaign. Enlistment centers throughout the nation were swamped with tens of thousands of men and women eager to join our armed forces. The reasons for this enormous groundswell in patriotic fervor were as follows:

First was the American soldier's love of country and its principles and the fact that our military personnel understood thoroughly all the correct reasons as to what they were fighting for. This was the main incentive that provided our armed forces with total loyalty to our country's cause.

Second was our country's drive and its willpower to impart to our military why this particular war was just. The Axis powers continually used methods of fear and harsh reprisals in their attempt to achieve loyalty. This loyalty would falter, and ultimately Axis armies would lose the motivation necessary for victory.

Pearl Harbor

Do you remember, everyone,
That fateful day in '41?
The enemy on that hateful day
Thought they'd have the final say.

Convinced we were an easy mark,
Those first few months things sure looked dark.
But six months later, we had our way,
Off Midway Island, we made them pay.

The Army, Navy, plus some Marines,
Helped MacArthur reclaim the Philippines;

And our great support from folks back home
Gave the reason to write this poem.
—The author

My own experience as a United States Marine commenced by being sworn in at the induction center in downtown New York City. After taking the oath of allegiance, I took the mandatory step forward under the direction of a Marine officer. After the necessary paperwork was completed, we enlistees were escorted to buses and ferries across the Hudson River and boarded a troop train, the Baltimore and Ohio, in Jersey City, New Jersey. With no air-conditioning, the train was stiflingly hot, making the trip extremely uncomfortable, especially with all that coal dust entering the open windows.

We arrived at Parris Island, South Carolina, on the second day. We enlistees boarded very large flatbed trucks, which drove us directly into the training camp. As our vehicles made their way slowly through the campsite, a persistent, loud chorus from hundreds of recruits that were doing close order drill echoed constantly until we reached our barracks. All one could hear over and over was "You'll be sorry!"

Our basic training at Parris Island lasted for eight weeks. Since it was early September, the days were very hot and humid, with close order drill and rifle calisthenics a daily, monotonous, boring routine. Temperatures often climbed into the nineties and occasionally caused some of the men to pass out while we were doing close order drill. Surprisingly, I seemed to withstand the rigorous training very well, believing that all the manual labor on our small farm prepared me well.

All trainees were constantly subjected to biting criticisms from our drill instructors when our marching performance did not meet with their rigid standards. It often occurred to me that the early European kings, centuries ago, endowed with divine rights, probably had less authority and influence than our own drill instructors, whose powers over us seemed more absolute. At least citizens under the king's rule could occasionally rely on royalty's noblesse oblige.

Blues in the Night

Those lazy, quiet summer days of 1942,
With all those foolish movie shows
Of marines dressed in blues.

With the chance I'll soon be drafted,
Not wanting to get shafted;
And those blue uniforms so well crafted,
I enlisted, never once procrasted.

Now I'll soon be all in clover,
With my dress blues I'll be a rover;
Though it never once occurred to me,
How soon my ass went overseas.
—The author

One weird punishment I will never forget took place during our training. It just so happened that instead of me shaving at six a.m. before morning inspection, I thought to myself, *why not shave at night*; after all, I did not have a heavy beard, and this way, I could save the time. Well, somehow, our eagle-eyed drill instructor felt my face in our morning inspection and detected a slight stubble. He asked me directly if I had shaved that morning. I guess I should have lied, because he sent me back to the barracks to return with my razor, and along with some other poor recruit, he had us face each other in front of the platoon dry-shaving each other. After that embarrassment and pain, I made sure to shave regularly each morning.

Another one of my trials and tribulations occurred during one of our lengthy arduous close order drill sessions in brutal summer heat. While our platoon was standing at attention, a mosquito lit on my cheek. Of course, the damn thing started biting me. I attempted to brush it off as quickly as possible, but the drill instructor caught me slapping at the insect. He stuck his face only an inch from mine and bellowed, "You were supposed to be at attention, mate!" Recoiling in fear, all I could do was meekly reply that I had brushed off a mosquito. "I don't give a good God damn if a bumblebee landed on you. When you are at attention, you stay that way, get it?" "Aye aye, sir!" I meekly replied.

Using the palm of his hand, the drill instructor slapped me on the head, which pushed the pith helmet I was wearing well below my eyes. When I attempted to straighten it out so I could see, the DI wouldn't allow me to touch it. When he gave the command to "forward march" with so many other quick commands, I had to look down at the ground in order to see where I was going. Calling the platoon to halt, the DI once again approached me and started chewing me out for looking down.

Reaching down, the drill instructor grabbed for my bayonet and drew it from its scabbard. With the handle of the bayonet shoved under my cartridge belt, the sharp point of the blade was not less than an inch from under my chin. He then gave the order to "forward march!" I could not see where I was going with my pith helmet still covering my eyes, but if I dared to even look down, the pointed end of the bayonet would have skewered me. Just how I continued to function with all of those continuous commands remains a total mystery for me.

After we left Parris Island by train after eight weeks of basic training, another two weeks were to be spent at Camp Lejeune, North Carolina, for advanced training in order to qualify on the rifle range with the new M1 Garand rifle. With three days of instruction on our new weapon in order to familiarize us, we became very proficient with it. Each morning, hundreds of marines would march out after breakfast to a large field. While taking several positions such as the kneeling, sitting, or prone positions, we would simulate firing at random targets. All one could hear were the thousands of clicks as each man pulled the trigger from those different positions. This monotonous routine would go on for hours on end.

This daily routine and its boredom was broken up one morning with a very unusual incident. During breakfast, one of the items served was ham and scrambled eggs. It just so happened that a year before entering the service, I had a bad experience with some ham in a New York restaurant. As I passed through the chow line, somehow the color of the ham just did not look very appetizing to me, so I just had the pancakes and cold cereal instead.

Within fifteen or twenty minutes, during our dry shooting exercises, hundreds of recruits were keeling over and began screaming in agony. All those marines who had eaten the ham and eggs were having attacks of ptomaine poisoning. Within minutes a dozen or more ambulances were carting the poor guys away to our local infirmaries. Had it not been for the bad experience in that N.Y. restaurant, no doubt, I would have suffered the same fate.

After ten days of our dry shooting routine, we moved into new barracks near the rifle range, where we would now be firing live ammunition. It would take five more days to prepare for rifle qualification. Each marine had an instructor-coach giving us the necessary instructions on how to attain the best results with our new M1. In our practice shooting, the instructor would constantly remind us by whispering in our ear to squeeze the trigger, before each round was fired. One of the more difficult positions for most of us was the sitting position. The troublesome part involved placing the right leg under your buttocks while having to sit on the ankle for proper balance. This difficult position, especially for many of the heavier guys, could be quite painful unless one was a contortionist.

Our instructors were primarily interested in having each man hit his target in a small pattern without having the shots spread all over the target. Of course, a bull's-eye was fine, but if your hits on the target was too spread out, God help you. The rangemaster, using binoculars, would occasionally sound off over the PA at some hapless marine, chastising him by calling out to that individual with typical sarcasm, "All right, that man on target number two, fix bayonets and charge!" Or something like "Those men on targets four and five, that's a fine group you have, you can cover it with a poncho!" I myself qualified twice, once as a sharpshooter and once as a marksman. I guess all the rabbit and quail hunting on the farm finally paid off.

Upon completing all categories in advanced training, every marine noted a complete change in our DI's attitude toward us. The change was welcomed by the men. No longer referred to as "boots," we finally were recognized as full-fledged marines. As it happened, I came down with an illness referred to as cat fever, with a temperature over 101. I was in the hospital for some five or six days and put on sulfur drugs. It was this short illness in the hospital that prevented me from being assigned to a unit like the rest of the men in our platoon; instead, I was sent to a casualty company to await reassignment.

After two weeks with nothing better to do but work details, I was becoming bored and decided I'd try to get into the paramarines. I walked into the office of a parachute battalion, and a marine captain looked up inquiring as to what I wanted. I told the captain I was awaiting reassignment in a casualty company, and I asked if it would be possible for me to get into the paramarines. Looking me up and down, the captain asked how much I weighed. I replied, "about 135 pounds, sir!" The captain's answer was very direct. "Go out and put on ten pounds, then come back and see me."

The last week of October, I received new orders and reported to my new unit, a weapons company in the Twenty-First Regiment, Third Marine Division. This newly formed division was receiving many replacements in order to build it up to full strength. Being somewhat shy, I was pleased with my acceptance into the new company. Not normally gregarious, I was naturally a little apprehensive.

Our training schedule in the company was very light, with just a few short hikes. The division at this time was readying itself and was already in the process of moving to the West Coast. We broke camp by mid-November, and I enjoyed the new experience aboard the troop trains' sleeping cars. The food aboard was very good and adequately portioned; the porters were very hospitable. The trip to California took five days, two days alone to cross Texas. While doing guard duty one night, I was standing on the boarding platform between the two cars when one of the train's porters passed by me. Looking warily at me holding a submachine gun, he inquired, "Is that gun loaded?" "Of course it's loaded!" I replied. "Well, what are you doing with that big gun anyway? You're nothing but a baby!" "What do you mean, a baby, I'm nineteen years old," I snapped back.

Arriving in California a week before Thanksgiving, we stayed at a navy camp called Camp Eliot. Shortly after arriving at this navy base, I was offered a two-week furlough. Most of the men received their leave at Camp Lejeune, and we replacements who arrived in the company late as I did were happy to be offered it now.

Having received my back pay of $80.00, it was necessary for me to inquire how much the train ticket would cost from

Los Angeles to New York. The round-trip fare was $70.60. This of course would leave me approximately ten dollars from my eighty-dollar paycheck. In order to have enough money for the five-day trip back to New York, I resigned myself to have only one meal per day. But it never occurred to me how expensive railroad dining car food could be. Within two days, my original ten dollars dwindled to just over five dollars.

Curious to see what was going on in some of the other cars, I passed some Air Corps personnel playing poker and politely asked if I might get into the game. I had already made the decision to risk losing the last five dollars; if I lost, I would have to exist on the free coffee and doughnuts the Red Cross women passed out at the railroad stations along the way. But the Gods smiled down on me, and the small ten- to twenty-cent poker game netted me over twenty dollars in winnings. With three more days before reaching New York, without even realizing I needed cab fare in Chicago since it was necessary to change railroad stations, I felt that someone was really watching over me.

Sitting up in coach for five days was arduous, but I finally arrived in New York City. My aunt invited me to stay at her apartment for the next few days. It was amazing the dozens of curious stares I received on the New York subways and in the streets. Apparently few people at that time saw marines, and they seemed perplexed trying to identify what military outfit my olive-green uniform stood for. When I passed army personnel on the streets, they saluted me, making my new status pleasing.

The family greeted me with open arms and asked dozens of questions relating to the war. All I could say was that I expected to be shipped overseas shortly.

After five days on leave, I took the subway to Penn Station, accompanied by my dad. I remember trying to reassure him that with the fine training I had received that he was not to worry. We both had watery eyes when I boarded the train to the West Coast. Having previously arranged for a monthly allotment deduction from my paycheck payable to my aunt, this naturally enabled me to return to the West Coast with a little more than the ten dollars I originally left California with.

Upon arriving back at Camp Eliot after five days and nights on the train, I learned from the officer of the day that the entire battalion was on landing maneuvers off the coast. Although I received instructions as to how I would find my outfit, it wasn't easy to locate my company late at night, so I questioned a dozen or more marines in other units. I finally located my company dug in on the approaches to the beach. As I approached, I was challenged by no other than my company commander. "Put out that God-damn flashlight!" he bellowed. "Mate, do you want to get your head shot off?" This was an attempt to remind me that if a potential enemy was in the area, that could have happened. The next morning I participated in the landing maneuvers, and much to my surprise, the morning along the beach was unusually cold for Southern California.

By the last week of January 1943, our company moved into the brand new marine base of Camp Pendleton. This enormous complex seemed to stretch for miles. Our stay would only be temporary, with rumors that our regiment would be leaving for overseas duty by the middle of February. We were given preprinted postcards with our new post office address typed in, so we could notify our families by mail after we left for overseas.

On February 14, 1943, we began our departure for overseas by boarding the 25,000-ton liner *Lurline*, a prewar luxury liner that made vacation cruises to Hawaii. Elements of the Twenty-First Regiment, plus other attached units aboard, cast off on February 15 from San Diego harbor for New Zealand. We left without any naval escort; because of the ship's speed, the navy felt that no enemy sub could catch us. When our ship crossed the equator, all troops aboard were called "Shell Backs." Those who had never crossed the equator had to go through a timeworn ritual. One by one, each man was dunked into a large tub of saltwater and slapped on the rear end with a flat wooden paddle. Boy, did that sting! The scene on the ship's deck looked more like a riot than anything else, as some of the more unpopular guys got chased down until caught.

One of the duties I happened to catch was to stand guard with binoculars, scanning the ocean for enemy submarines, on one of the ship's gun turrets, which was manned by a navy crew on the very top of the ship. It never occurred to me with those ocean breezes blowing so briskly, to put on a shirt. Being so close to the equator and on a four-hour watch, I incurred a nasty sunburn that needed medical attention. The fascinating sights on board were to watch the dolphins, flying fish, and the albatrosses, sailing overhead so effortlessly. Fortunately, in the thirteen days it took us to reach New Zealand, there was not one submarine scare.

Before leaving the United States, I had read an article in the *Reader's Digest* about Captain Eddie Rickenbacker, the famous fighter pilot in World War I, and how the passenger plane with him and several others made a forced landing in the Pacific Ocean. Stranded in a life raft approximately thirty days with little food or water, only a few survived the ordeal. Remembering that tragic article, just a few days before leaving the States, I purchased several fishhooks and line at a local sports store, anticipating that in case our troopship met a similar fate, I would at least have this fishing line in an emergency. However, little did I realize at the time how important the fishing line I had purchased would ultimately be to me during the Bougainville campaign.

New Zealand

Arriving in Auckland Harbor, New Zealand, on March 1, after a quiet, routine voyage of thirteen days, our regiment disembarked in the harbor's bustling city of Auckland. With all units dressed in full combat gear, our Twenty-First Regiment marched down the city's main wide thoroughfare toward the railroad station. What an impressive sight we must have been! The city's population turned out by the thousands, lining the streets and sidewalks with unabashed cheering.

Without a doubt, the men were overwhelmed by this enthusiastic reception. Our troop train took about an hour to arrive at our destination, a small railroad station five or six miles from a quaint little town called Warkworth. After being loaded aboard large trucks, it took us only ten minutes to reach our new campsite. We must have passed thousands of sheep on the way, feeding on the sloping green pastures. The campsite had small wooden huts lined up row upon row, with barely enough room inside for six sleeping cots.

It took us a few days to get organized, and we knew that we would be in for an extensive training program. After adjusting to our new surroundings, we started in on ten-mile conditioning hikes in preparation for the sixty-mile hikes we were to be taking in the ensuing weeks. In the weeks that followed, an extensive training program was in force: night marches, field problems, anti-tank and anti-aircraft firing, along with scouting and organized athletics. The organized athletics were mandatory, with baseball and touch football sessions. The men always referred to these as "organized grab-ass!" With all the strenuous training programs, all we wanted to do was to sack out in our cots.

We had to engage in early morning calisthenics by using our rifles in a cadenced routine, stretching our torsos in every conceivable position as our platoon leaders bellowed commands of "muzzles up, muzzles down, butts up, butts down," over and over again. Appropriately, we called these exercises physical torture under the armpits. I myself, always half asleep, would often manage to stand in the last row behind the tallest marine so that our platoon leader could not see me. This somewhat hidden location allowed me to feign the motions halfheartedly. Those early morning exercise sessions were one of the necessary evils of military life foisted upon us that seemed to annoy us to the very brink of distemper.

One of several methods we used to break the boredom on our long hikes was to sing popular songs, which often helped lift our morale. Our favorite little ditty, probably because of its inspirational anti-service connotation, was this clever little tune.

They wake you up at five o'clock in the morning,
for fifty dollars a day, once a month,
They take us on a hike without any warning,
for fifty dollars a day, once a month,
Your feet will hurt, your back will break, and you'll be muscle bound,
But all of that will disappear
when payday comes around,
For seven days a week, they build up your physique,
for fifty dollars a day, once a month.

As usual, we always looked forward to Sundays. Given the day off, most of the men went on liberty to Auckland. The salary for a private was sixty dollars a month; that included the 20 percent overseas pay. Arriving in Auckland by train around ten a.m., we were amazed that in order for us to cash our U.S. currency in exchange for New Zealand currency, we had to make the exchange in their banks. The local small businesses never seemed to have enough money in their cash registers to break our twenty-dollar bills. Half the population must have thought we were millionaires.

Most of our time was spent on touring the city, going to the local dances, and taking in the many restaurants, especially at the hotels. Amazingly, one could have a complete steak dinner for under one U.S. dollar. Our money went such a long way, it was surprising to us how long our original twenty dollars lasted. Curfew time was at ten p.m. The lovers who did not make it back to camp in time were considered over leave, and the punishment was for the next five days to live in a dirt floor tent on bread and water, appropriately named by the men as "piss and punk."

Having lost most of my money in a poker game one week, I unfortunately had to forego my liberty one Sunday and decided to partake in a little fishing expedition. Some days before, I had noticed only a short distance behind our campsite a very nice stream that had some areas that looked fairly deep, especially where a large tree bordered it. Having been an avid fisherman back in New Jersey, I took the fishing line and hooks I had purchased and attached the hook after finding what looked like a pretty deep hole in the bend of the stream, with the roots of a very large tree bordering it.

Pulling up a large clump of soil, I grabbed a juicy worm, baited the hook, and threw the drop line into the deepest part of the stream. I didn't have to wait but a few seconds before I had one helluva tug on the line. Whatever it was, it fought like hell and felt real hefty. Pulling half of the thing out of the water, I was staring into the eyes of an enormous black eel as thick as my forearm. Damn! I have seen many an ugly fish in my day. When I looked into those beady black eyes and sharp white teeth just inches from my face, I let out a shriek, dropped the fishing line with the eel still hooked, and hightailed it back to camp as fast as my skinny legs would carry me.

I thought it best, out of curiosity, to find out just what was in that stream. One of the local town's citizens told me that many of the eels in these streams live for many years and grow to enormous sizes. He also cautioned me about wading barefoot, as if I needed to be reminded. I told him that "the stream had seen the very last of me."

At a company formation, our C.O. told us that our entire regiment would be making a sixty-mile hike shortly that would last for three days. This was naturally greeted with very little enthusiasm, inasmuch as our units had made only a few short hikes. A forced march of sixty miles we all felt would be a disaster without enough shorter conditioning hikes to toughen us up for the long one. Forced marches allow a ten-minute break for every sixty minutes of marching; and even though we would carry full canteens of water, a strict water discipline rule would be in effect. Someone had suggested placing a small pebble under our tongues, which was supposed to suppress the desire for water; for me at least, it worked out very well.

In company formation, the men lined up just after breakfast, which consisted of powdered eggs, French toast, and coffee. Carrying our packs, which weighed approximately forty pounds, plus our rifles and steel helmets, we commenced moving out just after six a.m., admittedly with some trepidation. After marching about four hours or so, the additional weight in our packs started having its effect, not to mention that many stretches of the hard gravel roads had as much as a thirty-degree incline and stretched uphill at least half a mile before reaching the top.

Every ten-minute break became more of a hindrance than a help. After four hours of marching, we experienced leg and foot pains, including lower back stiffness from the additional weight in our packs. We needed help from one of our men to pull each of us up after each break. By six p.m., after covering twenty-six miles, orders were given to us to pitch our two-man pup tents on a sloping sheep pasture. Many men already needed medical attention from our corpsmen for the blisters on their feet, a precursor we felt of things yet to come.

The second day of the forced march became a veritable fiasco. Hundreds of men were forced out of the hike by painful blisters. Many had to be taken by ambulances back to their respective camps. But in spite of our discomfort, we could not help but take notice of the beautiful countryside and the attractive, well-constructed homes along the roadsides. So often, the residents of these lovely homes came out to welcome us with pitchers of fresh cold milk. New Zealand's people were the friendliest and kindest we had ever met.

On the third day into our march, I estimated at least 50 percent of the regiment were unable to continue, due mainly to having sore feet and blisters. Try as I could, my feet badly blistered, forcing me to discontinue, and I fell out of line after forty-eight miles. The top brass knew that several more conditioning hikes would have to be made, inasmuch as it had been only three weeks since we arrived in New Zealand. Six weeks after our first attempt, a second sixty-miler was a complete success.

It was on that first sixty-mile hike that an unusual incident happened that today still remains an enigma for me. On the second day of the hike, late in the day while I was preparing my pup tent for the evening, two men in our platoon called to me and said they wanted to ask me a question. When I approached them, they asked me point-blank, "Say, Friedman, is anyone in our company giving you a hard time?" Although I thought the question a little unusual, I quickly answered that I had no problems with anyone in the outfit. "Why do you both ask?" I inquired. "Well, if anyone in the outfit gives you a hard time, just let us know," they replied.

These men were close buddies. Because of their size and stature in our unit, they always took it upon themselves to act as enforcers in whatever way they personally perceived as necessary to prevent any disharmony when minor disruptions occasionally occurred within the confines of our company. No one seemed to mind their roles as peacemakers because when disruptive situations arose that needed mediation, these two seemed to be eminently fair and well qualified for the job.

Returning to my pup tent, I was mystified as to why I was singled out for any protection from them. Known in the company as a loner, I often kept to myself in that I rarely created any waves. Thinking the situation over, I came to the conclusion that had I accepted their offer of protection, I would become their errand boy; my rejection of their offer was my way of maintaining my independence.

One of the more interesting training activities was a visit to one of New Zealand's army camps. After a twenty-mile trip by truck, we had the rare privilege of inspecting some of their beach fortifications, which looked to me very formidable. Later that afternoon, their personnel invited us for lunch in their mess hall, challenging us to a baseball game after lunch. Baseball is not one of their national sports, and we won decisively. But in a game of cricket, I know the odds would have been in their favor.

Every month or so, the officers in our company arranged to have a busload or two of girls from the surrounding towns and villages visit our campsite. Our mess hall was set up as a dance floor, with a buffet table set up along with a variety of cakes and refreshments that made a very nice homelike atmosphere. It was a very nice way to meet these lovely young ladies, and some of our men became romantically involved—even meeting some of their families.

Of course, one of the strict rules imposed by our officers at the dance was that we were not permitted to leave the dance floor or the building with any of the ladies. Never one for not stretching the rules a bit, I somehow managed to avoid being seen leaving the building with one of the pretty girls. As it was already dark outside, with both of us already some distance from the dance, we both decided to sit down and relax in the tall grass.

To my pleasant surprise, the young lady became quite receptive to my advances and, being dark, I felt I was given a green light to pursue the relationship a little further. Oblivious to any noise or sound, we did not hear approaching footsteps coming toward us. Suddenly a flashlight shone upon us, and I immediately leaped to my feet to confront this intruder. This intruder pretended to be an officer, demanding to know what we were doing outside. When he asked to see my ID, I became suspicious; because of his limited intellect and youthful face, I confronted him with a challenge to his authority. From his sheepish grin, I surmised correctly that he was a fraud and proceeded to chew him out for his untimely interruption. Slightly shaken, the young lady and I returned to the dance with no one being the wiser.

A day or so later, our platoon was designated to fire our .50 caliber machine guns at a target sleeve drawn behind an old biplane. Our vehicles were lined up along a very high cliff overlooking the ocean. As the target sleeve would safely come into view, we would fire at it from the back of trucks, which had our .50 caliber weapons mounted on them. Every man was given an opportunity to fire at the target sleeve. When it came my turn, one of my bursts struck the towline and the target sleeve fell into the ocean. Our C.O. in disgust shouted, "That's it for today, men, it will take much too long for that plane to return with another sleeve!" *Just one of those days*, I thought to myself. It seems I just can't win for losing. I briefly thought I might receive a well done, nice shooting pat on the back, but the look on our C.O.'s face dispelled that thought.

All of the extensive training the past few months rapidly came to an end. By June, the top brass felt the men were ready for bigger and better things. The consensus among our men seemed to agree. In July, our third battalion boarded ship, and we left beautiful New Zealand on the transport ship *George Clymer*. After a submarine scare or two, our ship pulled into Noumea Harbor, New Caledonia, for one day. The trip from there to Guadalcanal took about three days. Arriving off Guadalcanal, we were ordered to unload the ship very quickly because of the frequent Japanese air raids. Working around the clock, we unloaded the ship in record time.

Guadalcanal

British Solomon Islands

The Solomon Islands chain, of which Honiara on Guadalcanal is the capital, has the largest population. The island chain that lies about one thousand miles northeast of Australia was governed by Great Britain from the late 1890s until 1978. The chain has a population of nearly 500,000 people, covering over 230,000 square miles.

There is a parliamentary democracy with a prime minister and a governor general, who represents the British monarchy in the Solomon chain. Its people are dark-skinned and called Melanesians. Their official language is English, although dozens of other languages are spoken, including Pidgin English. Volcanoes formed the island's mountains, and some are still active. The main products of the island's economy are fish, timber, and palm oil, most of which Japan purchases.

The island's climate is hot and humid, with an annual rainfall of over 100 inches. Air routes connect it with Australia, which exports machinery and a variety of manufactured goods to the islands. A weekly newspaper is in English, and radio broadcasts are also in English.

Coconut Grove Campsite

Driven by truck about five miles inland, we started setting up camp on an enormous coconut tree plantation nearly two miles square that was capable of encamping our entire Third Marine Division. The difficult, tedious job of pitching tents in long rows between the coconut trees naturally took precedence. Guadalcanal in July 1943 was perfectly secure, except for the night air raids during the moonlit nights from the thirteenth to the seventeenth of the month when the moon was at its brightest. On those full moon nights, enemy bombers would come over at very high altitudes to bomb us, which made it very difficult for our anti-aircraft defenses to reach them at a height over 20,000 feet.

Guadalcanal Campaign

Pre-Invasion Summary 1942

When our naval reconnaissance aircraft discovered an enemy airstrip under construction on Guadalcanal shortly after the Coral Sea battle in April 1942, our navy's high command knew this new airstrip would imperil our vital lifelines to Australia. Plans were quickly drawn up to invade Guadalcanal, with the invasion date set for August 7, 1942, using the First Marine Division in the initial invasion known as operation Watchtower, dubbed "Shoestring" because of the tenuous conditions. In the six-month campaign, ship losses on both sides were very high.

Japanese naval forces, in just one night attack off the island of Savo, sunk four of our heavy cruisers: *Vincennes, Quincy, Canberra,* and *Astoria.* Shortly thereafter, we lost the cruisers *San Francisco, Northhampton, Helena, Juneau, Chicago,* and *San Juan,* not to mention the aircraft carriers *Wasp* and *Hornet*, and the 35,000-ton *North Carolina* was badly damaged.

The tragic loss of these fine ships severely jeopardized our entire land operations on Guadalcanal. Our Marine units ashore became so untenable that Admiral Ghormley was replaced by none other than Admiral "Bull" Halsey. It was Halsey's bold, brilliant strategy that saved our land forces from that logistical nightmare by taking on in full measure powerful Japanese sea power in the Solomon Islands. Victory was complete by finally securing Guadalcanal on February 9, 1943.

A Veteran's Lament

In the vastness of blue ocean depths,
Sleep good men and fine ships
we dare not forget;
They stood proud and brave
in our country's cause,
In noblest tradition
they would act without pause.
They'll never mention their stories from
the deep ocean main,
Mark these words, one and all ...
sinful wars are to blame.
Marked feats during battle,
they asked no favor,
With backs to the wall,
never once did they waver;

A love for our country,
so notably signified,
The price they all paid
would hopefully be justified.
Obvious wrongs we prayed
would be righted,

But our dreams have long passed
by a memory blighted;
So dwell not, old soldier,
this happened before.
Who will pick up the mantle
to settle a score?
—The author

As for our own Third Marine Division, Guadalcanal proved to be an excellent jungle training ground, and our training was intensified as the weeks went by. On one of the many night training problems, our platoon chose an open area to set up our pup tents alongside the Balasuma River. This wide-open area with smooth stones that lined both sides of the river gave us a great view of the rich black starlit sky. About eleven p.m., we could hear the island's air-raid sirens go off in the distance. Lying flat on our backs with our upper packs as pillows, we could see the distant searchlights crisscrossing the clear starlit sky trying to pick up the enemy formation flying at an extremely high altitude. Suddenly one of the enemy bombers became caught in our searchlights and was lit up like a bright jewel by at least three or more searchlight beams.

Our anti-aircraft batteries were ineffective because the bombers were much too high for our anti-aircraft guns to reach them. Suddenly, in full view of us in that black velvet sky, a stream of red tracer bullets from one of our night fighters found its mark and the enemy bomber burst into flames. Completely enveloped in fire, as it was falling it seemed to veer toward us. In minutes, this flaming hulk passed over us by only a thousand feet or so and crashed into the jungle less than a mile from where we were lying. Guadalcanal is over sixty miles long, and for this flaming mass to come so close and almost smash into us casually resting there was scary as hell.

Those air raids were made only on the nights that were full moon, between the thirteenth and seventeenth of August through October. Around one or two a.m., several raids were made by a lone enemy bomber, just to harass us and keep us awake. These lone air raiders were nicknamed "Washing Machine Charley," because of the uneven drone of their engines. The annoyance of getting into our foxholes and the loss of sleep was a little irritating, but those lone night raiders rarely would drop any bombs.

On one other "Washing Machine Charley" raid, as we lay in our foxholes, someone in the Regimental Headquarters area neglected to turn off their Coleman lantern a minute or so after the air-raid sirens went off. After some anxious minutes, with that bright light still burning, someone in a foxhole just behind me bellowed out in a loud roar that could be heard and probably reverberated throughout the entire regimental area, "Put that God damn light out, you son of a bitch, before I shoot it out!" It only took a few moments, and the light was turned off. We all breathed a sigh of relief.

Next morning the entire battalion was ordered to make a twenty-mile hike with full packs and rifles. How come, we all wondered, because this hike was not on our training schedule. The mystery was solved when we found out that the lantern momentarily left on last night belonged to our own regimental commander, and the twenty-mile hike was our punishment for that loud outburst. No one would own up as to who the loudmouthed culprit was.

Our Coconut Grove campsite was very well set up and things were fairly cozy, except for the heavy tropical rains that deluged our camp every so often. But the thousands of coconut trees would soak up the rainwater, and the foot or so of water would disappear in a few hours. The food on Guadalcanal was fair, with frozen mutton from Australia being the only meat available. The meat, of course, had to have its flavor well camouflaged in order to mask its terrible aroma, but it all depended on just how good the company cook was or what the cook's daily disposition was on that particular day.

Sundays on Guadalcanal were days off for all of us. Most of the men washed their fatigues, wrote letters, tidied up their tents, or just relaxed from the hectic training schedule. As for me, after taking care of my personal chores, I hitched a ride to the beach only five minutes away. Inasmuch as there were practically no women from our own services on the island, we men could swim bare-assed on Guadalcanal's beaches, a freedom we all came to appreciate.

On this particular lovely Sunday afternoon, after stripping down, I swam out to a raft about one hundred feet offshore. Lying on my stomach, I could see small schools of fish under the raft casually swimming while I took in the sun and occasionally studied the fascinating coastline of the island. Suddenly I heard the sound of a plane, seemingly close by. While scanning the coastline, I noticed it was one of our own B-25s, lazily circling over the beach at a very low altitude.

Somehow I sensed that the plane's crew had spotted me on the raft, naked as a jaybird. My premonition was correct because the bomber commenced making a wide circle. As I watched in awe, it started making a beeline for me. When it roared over the raft, I estimated the twin-engine monster had to be about thirty feet over my head, forcing me to drop flat on my stomach. Wow, was I terrified! I could easily envision the plane's crew roaring with laughter at my distress. Jumping to my feet, all I could do was wave my fist at them and scream at the top of my lungs the worst profanities I could think of. No doubt about it, had I brought along my M1 rifle, I would have pumped all eight rounds into that B-25 and to hell with the consequences.

On one of the many training exercises we held, our platoon drove our 37mm anti-tank weapons down to the beach for one of our scheduled firing sessions. This time we fired at a wooden target sled that had three fifty-gallon drums attached to it being pulled by one of the landing craft some five to six hundred yards offshore. Of course, the target was to simulate a moving tank, and each anti-tank weapon would fire individually trying to destroy it.

As the sled came into firing view, each gun would open fire. With little success so far, we were scoreless. When it came my turn to fire, my first shot was a direct hit, and the target sled was totally obliterated. What amazed everyone was that it usually takes a few rounds just to get the proper range and lead on the target. When the target was towed in, it wasn't even repairable. Our C.O. gave me one of those disdainful looks, but begrudgingly gave me a belated "nice shot, Friedman!" and announced that our target practice had ended for the day. The raft would have taken too long to repair. I felt that temporarily I had become persona non grata; but as the good Lord would have it, I would have another chance to redeem myself in the eyes of our C.O.

Some days later, my squad sergeant informed me that he and I were chosen to give a firing demonstration with our 37mm gun for several high-ranking Army, Navy, Marine, and Australian officers. We were taken to a special firing range, where cardboard silhouette targets were set up between thirty and sixty yards away, placed about twenty feet apart. With the top brass looking on, my squad sergeant and I were told to fire this special canister ammunition at the set up targets as fast as we could and not worry about taking time to aim. These instructions came directly from our own C.O. Canister shells have hundreds of pea-sized lead shot inside, and the purpose was to see just how many hits could be made on the targets without taking the normal time to carefully aim.

Japanese infantry, according to reports from recent battles, were making full-scale frontal assaults against our frontline positions. By ascertaining how many hits were made on our targets, our top brass could estimate how effective this new canister ammunition would be against mass enemy infantry assaults on our units. When our firing was over, the officers inspected the targets and seemed very pleased with the results. The C.O. gave my squad sergeant and myself a well-done nod, and hopefully this time, I would be out of the doghouse for destroying that wooden raft.

Every Sunday was a new experience for me on Guadalcanal. One of my favorite pastimes was to take my M1 and wade upstream in the Balasuma River. The water was always very clear, only three or four feet deep or less in most places, making it easy to navigate. Taking three or four clips of ammo, I could shoot at anything that looked tempting. Following the river's course inland up to three miles, I would shoot at schools of fish, an occasional snake, or at some large bird well off in the distance.

After wending my way upriver for well over a mile, I ran into four or five of the island's natives. The Solomon Islanders are very dark-skinned but are quite fluent in English. I noticed they were attempting to climb one of the coconut trees, so I asked if they would let me shoot some of coconuts down for them and save them the trouble of climbing; they readily agreed. After I fired into the large clusters of coconuts, several fell down and the natives beamed with delight.

I offered them an opportunity to fire my weapon, but they declined. I then offered to give them a firing demonstration instead. Placing an object on a tree trunk, I proceeded to demonstrate my skill. The target was only fifty to sixty yards away, so it wasn't very difficult for me to make short work of the coconut I placed there. When I offered them a second chance to fire my weapon, two of the natives agreed, but made no hits. As I finished off the target, they grinned with delight. Picking up their coconuts, they waved a friendly goodbye and disappeared into the jungle, and I continued on my merry way upstream.

I was now deep into the interior of the island, and the heat was starting to get to me. I sat down on the river's embankment, with my rifle cradled across my lap, my mind a million miles away to thoughts of home. Out of the corner of my eye, about one hundred feet to my left, a teenaged native girl was crossing the stream toward my side. Damn, I thought, was I hallucinating? Was she a mirage? I stared in disbelief as the teenager stopped in the middle of the stream, lifted her skirt, and with a cupped hand, started splashing water at the crotch between her legs.

I could see her eyes watching me, but the girl did not turn her head toward me. Needless to say, just about every crazy thought went racing through my mind. However, my better judgment prevailed. After crossing to my side, the teenager continued on her way without so much as a single word passing between us.

One of the familiar sites on Guadalcanal in 1943 were the heavy bomber formations as they approached the island from offshore. These B-24s were returning from their bombing raids on enemy bases. Very often one or more of the bombers in formation were smoking as they headed inland to land. In 1943, Japanese bases were heavily fortified with anti-aircraft weapons and were a veritable hornet's nest of enemy fighters that would rise en masse to attack our bomber formations.

As I watched this flight of returning B-24s from the beach one Sunday, one of the smoking bombers broke formation. With all that heavy smoke pouring from it, I knew the plane was in serious trouble. As it lost altitude, it passed over me standing there on the beach. Stricken with horror, I saw it crash into the jungle a mile or so away. The impact and massive ball of flames indicated that it was fruitless for me to make it to the crash site.

The Solomon Islands were plagued with mosquitoes (anopheles) carrying malaria. For some reason, the islanders infected with malaria did not seem to suffer as much as we with this malady. I surmised that over many generations, the islanders built up a kind of immunity to malaria. One of the first orders given to us when we arrived on the island was to keep our shirtsleeves all the way down and keep our trouser pants tucked into our socks, especially after sunset. To be caught not doing so meant a reprimand at best and being bitten by the malaria mosquito at worst.

Late one afternoon, I ran out of my tent without taking the precautions of tucking in my trousers or rolling down my sleeves. As I crossed the company area, our executive officer stopped me cold. "Mate!" he yelled, "Why haven't you taken the necessary precautions?" I stood frozen in my tracks as the officer asked for my name. Much to my surprise, he did not know my name, even though I was in the unit for almost a year. He let me go with just a reprimand. It later occurred to me that making myself previously as inconspicuous as I possibly could, would in some ways have its benefits.

One of the methods during our stay on Guadalcanal to suppress malaria was to take Atabrine tablets. These little yellow pills were given to us, and we were strongly urged to take the Atabrine without fail. Somehow the rumor got around that these tablets would cause sterility, which was not true; with our skin taking on a yellowish appearance, it did not help to dispel the myth. Our officers found out that the men were quietly disposing of the tablets. The only way to remedy this was for each platoon to line up in formation while our platoon leaders placed the Atabrine pill on each man's tongue, making sure we would swallow them, thus ending that little deception.

On August 13, which happened to be a Friday, our third platoon was sent by truck to Lunga Point, where a mile offshore the cargo ship *John Penn* was anchored. We were formed into a working party of about thirty men and boarded the *John Penn* to unload 155mm artillery shells that were stored in the cargo hold. We started work at eight a.m. and were relieved at four p.m. by a fresh group of working party marines from another unit. Our encampment was only a half mile in from the beach; and when the air-raid sirens went off at nine p.m., everyone climbed into their foxholes to wait out the impending air raid.

This particular raid was very heavy; and the airfield, a short distance behind us, was literally devastated by the Japanese night raiders. By morning we found out that the *John Penn*, which we had unloaded earlier, was torpedoed and all hands went down with the ship, including those marines who had relieved us at four p.m.

The next morning we were detailed to pick up the floating bodies and bring them ashore for burial. Had my platoon started working at four p.m. instead of eight a.m., I do not think I would have survived that sinking. I've often wondered who the marine was who made out that working party manifest that assigned my platoon to unload the ship on the early eight a.m. shift. Yes, I believe God was with me and my third platoon that day. The information we received was that the enemy torpedo plane approached with its landing lights on. With the airfield so close by, the ship probably thought it was one of our own planes; the darkness made it difficult to identify.

The next day we returned to our camp at Coconut Grove and listened to Tokyo Rose on the shortwave radio in our jeep. In her typical oozing manner, she taunted us about that air raid and the damage it caused, but we were amused listening to her incessant lies and enjoyed the great popular music she always played for us. Our own psychological warfare came in the form of leaflets that encouraged Japanese soldiers to desert.

Translation of the Surrender Leaflet

To noncombatants:

We understand that you are experiencing great hardships living in the jungle for long periods of time. However, in the present situation, continued struggle is intolerable. At this juncture, for the next generation, we recommend you fling away all your emotions and obtain American's internment. Especially if you are sick, receive the treatment quickly. At the present time, over 200 men have chosen this path and they are all living with hope, honor and safety.

We wish you Japanese soldiers and the people in the nation to throw down weapons and come to us. You fought as hard as you can for the country. Now, resistance will be fatal. People who come to us will get food, clothing, shelter, tobacco, and an allowance. Otherwise, await death and suffering with illnesses and starvation in the jungle. Therefore, take the following steps to engage the American forces.

1. Take off your jackets, throw away your weapons, raise your hands and walk through the middle of the road toward a spot where Americans are present.

2. If you are on the coastline, show many flags. American battleships will take notice and render assistance.

Sept. 28
Komatsu Shigeru
Isoda Isao

Guard duty was just one of the necessary evils foisted on us enlisted men. Fortunately, it was given in alphabetical order that usually took at least four to six weeks before the duty came around to us again. For me at least, the worst shift was the two a.m. to six a.m. shift, which always afforded one the least amount of sleep. On one particular occasion, I was given this miserable shift of guarding our trucks and weaponry in our gun park. By four a.m. or so, I thought it would be safe for me to take a little snooze under one of our large trucks where I would be well hidden from the sergeant of the guard if and when he would make his rounds.

With our own squad sergeant as sergeant of the guard, I felt I would be safe. Well! I was dead wrong, and I was caught sound asleep under one of our trucks. Fortunately for me, I always had an excellent rapport with him, and being a good marine, he didn't bring me up on charges. Sleeping on watch is a very serious offense, and had it been one of our other officers, I might have had the book thrown at me. One of the benefits of doing KP duty was not doing guard duty during the thirty days served on KP. I often would volunteer for another month of KP just to avoid having to do guard duty.

Guadalcanal is separated from the Florida Islands by the Sealark Channel, which lies approximately twenty miles away. When Guadalcanal was bombed during those bright moonlit nights, Tulagi often came under simultaneous attack, so it was easy for us to see the bright bomb flashes and the loud delayed report when the bombs would explode. Tulagi was primarily a navy base, and when making landing maneuvers in the area, we could see many PT boats lined up neatly along the shoreline. It was here that Lt. John Kennedy and his now famous PT 109 operated up and down the Solomon Islands chain.

By the middle of September, every unit received orders to enclose our outhouses, urinals, and showers with tarpaulin, and strict orders were issued of no more swimming nude in the ocean. What the hell is going on here, we asked, and were finally informed that a very high female dignitary would be visiting Guadalcanal shortly. That dignitary was no other than Mrs. Eleanor Roosevelt. All those freedoms we took for granted were now gone, and the men were really pissed. Many of the area's high-ranking officers were also a little uneasy about her visit.

Although I did not see Mrs. Roosevelt personally, she made several visits to the island hospitals and greeted the sick and wounded. Mrs. Roosevelt took written letters from the men and promised she would faithfully get in touch with the families of the men she visited. As it turned out, Mrs. Roosevelt's visit became an excellent morale booster. Upon her return to the states, I'm sure she gave the President a substantial accounting of her Pacific tour.

NO SWEAT

There's no need for a lesson in math,
Because some guy's not taking a bath;
When there's no windy weather,
We all suffer together;
And the guilty deserve all our wrath.

We're lucky we don't pay any rent,
Since living is hell in a tent;
If you think it's terrific,
Here in the Pacific;
Even the flowers stay bent.

In the shower he pouts and he frowns,
Especially while holding him down;
We marines have our pride;
And don't wish to sound snide;
What else should we do with these clowns?
—The author

One of the drawbacks marines incurred was the secrecy that always surrounded our movements throughout the Pacific theatre. Our platoon leaders censored the letters to our families. And not a word of our whereabouts was permitted, making our letters less meaningful and informative to our families. As for me, my mail from home kept clamoring for some details about my location and whether I had participated in any of the fighting that the family was reading about. Any information, no matter how innocuous and seemingly insignificant, was cut away from our letters by our platoon leaders.

My mail from home kept incessantly reminding me of the fact that others in the armed forces were able to write home and provide their families information of their whereabouts while our mail remained so secretive about our locations. Finally, after continuous badgering from home for more information, I hit upon what I thought to be an ingenious plan. In my letters, I told the family how the high humidity caused the stamps to lose their stickiness and that I had to use gum in order to make the stamps stick to the envelopes. One of my letters advised the family to look under the gum, where I had written the word Guadalcanal. Of course, I thought the idea was foolproof, but my lieutenant smelled a rat and came into my tent asking me point-blank if I had written anything unauthorized under the gum.

Unwilling and frightened to admit the truth because of the penalty I thought I would have to incur, I replied negatively. The lieutenant looked straight at me as if I had placed something unauthorized under the gum. Whether the lieutenant believed me or not, I would never know. Ultimately, nothing more came of the incident, but rest assured, that was the last attempt I would make to break the code of secrecy.

In the ten months our Third Marine Division garrisoned Guadalcanal, we marines maintained a wonderful, friendly relationship with the island's native population. Regularly, the natives would come into our camps, either selling or bartering with us many of their handmade ornaments, such as hand carvings, grass skirts, and so on. All they asked for was one dollar for any item they had for sale. The natives also sought the unenviable job of laundering our clothes, and one could see them down at the river's front with those large bars of brown soap scrubbing away. All we had to do was hang our clothes out to dry for the mere price of two dollars. This, of course, would relieve us from that tedious, laborious job.

Guadalcanal's native population were given total access to our PX's and were often seen standing on line making purchases of pipes, tobacco, and lighter fluid. It was amazing to see them breaking out large wads of paper money, mostly singles, of course, accumulated from their weeks of doing our laundry. It was a rarity not to see them with a pipe in their mouths just puffing away. I don't know which was worse, the tobacco or the beetlewood they always chewed, which left a dark stain on their teeth that was so noticeable when they smiled.

One of the items we were very happy to barter for was our canned corned beef for their large stalks of bananas. It was no secret how we detested canned corned beef, and the islanders just loved it. One of the common sights was large stalks of bananas hanging in our tents; as they ripened, we would pluck one or two if we were lucky enough to get to it before the other men in the tent. The native men had a great sense of humor, and in some of our bantering sessions with them we would jokingly ask how we marines could get some "push-push." Never embarrassed, they unhesitatingly replied, "Uh, push-push not good! Make'em body not strong!" Of course, these humorous sessions were strictly in jest and just our way of having an innocent laugh with each other. Happily, they never appeared offended.

In prewar Guadalcanal, many of the island's native population were employed on large coconut plantations in the production of copra from the coconuts. I often wondered after we left the island, in May 1944, how the natives were able to return to their old jobs. With all the money they had accumulated while our forces were there, I felt that we had perhaps spoiled them; how difficult it would be for them to return to the lower wages they probably made on the copra plantations.

By October, our training started to intensify throughout the entire division. About ten men, including myself, were chosen to train our third battalion in order to accustom the men to having live ammunition fired over their heads. Ten of us boarded two trucks with all the necessary gear, including three .30 caliber machine guns. Traveling through the narrow jungle roads, the site chosen was a large clearing about three miles inland.

Every so often, some of us would cry out from the back of the truck "wait a minute!" Our vehicle would have to stop in order for us to remove the thorns from the hanging vines that penetrated our fatigues. Interestingly, this is how those vines received their "wait a minute" reputation.

We arrived at a very large clearing and set up our campsite and our .30 caliber machine guns in a semicircle around a large ravine. Each morning a full company of men would march out from their campsites in Coconut Grove and immediately climb down into the steep ravine. When they were positioned safely, we would fire live ammunition from our machine guns over their heads. The purpose was to familiarize them with live fire; this helped enable the men to determine the direction the machine gun fire was coming from.

This entire exercise took about one hour. The infantry company would climb up the steep slope, and the exercise was then over. By early afternoon, a second company would arrive and the same procedure would ensue. All we had to do then was clean down our weapons and place a light coat of oil on them.

This same procedure was repeated each day, and it would take at least a week or more before we would get around to doing the entire battalion. The rest of the day for us was free time, and some of us would take our rifles down to the river for some target practice while the other men would just relax playing cards, mostly blackjack.

On the second day, several of the local natives approached us and offered to trade with us their fresh corn and sweet potatoes, along with a live chicken, for our cans of corned beef. What a swap—our corned beef for their fresh veggies and a chicken! So, for dinner that afternoon, we boiled all the sweet corn and sweet potatoes in a metal container the ammunition came in. We also ate fried chicken, and what a feast it was. We were probably the only ones on Guadalcanal lucky enough to feast on fresh corn, sweet potatoes, and fried chicken. We doubted whether the top brass on the island had it that well.

The exercise took about ten days, and we were sorry to see it end. The officer in charge of our detail was Captain Clayton Rockmore, the C.O. from I Company; and for some reason, he took a liking to me. We had several informal talks, mainly about my civilian life. Interestingly, after the Bougainville campaign, he came into our camp and inquired as to how I was doing. He would do likewise after the Guam campaign. It was a devastating blow to me when I heard he was killed in action on Iwo Jima. I still remember how friendly he was—an easygoing, regular guy.

Shortly after those exercises, I came down with a very high fever. I reported to sick bay and found out I had malaria. The days spent on the machine gun exercise made many of us very lax about taking the precautions necessary from the vicious mosquitoes. Some of us paid the price. I was hospitalized with high fever and had intermittent chills; no matter how many blankets I covered myself with, I continued to tremble from the chills. I was given quinine each day and finally released in about six days.

With the Bougainville campaign now targeted for November 1, 1943, the usual amount of inoculations were given us for some of the prevalent diseases that this part of the world was well noted for. A series of five shots was given; and for some reason, I always seemed to suffer from these inoculations more than anyone else. True to form, after a few days one of the shot sites on my left arm, near the shoulder, became swollen. When the swelling and pain persisted, I reported to sick bay. Our company corpsman sent me over to the regimental infirmary, and the doctor examined me. The doctor informed me that it was probably either a dirty needle or that one of the shots was contaminated.

The doctor informed me I would have to wait until the swelling receded before it could be lanced and the poisonous fluid drained. "What!" I exclaimed in a loud voice, "What do you mean lanced? I have never been under a knife before, Doc! Won't this thing go away by itself?" "Son!" he said, "You either have that arm lanced or you will lose it!" "OK, Doc, you're the doctor!" I replied. It took another week before the swelling came down and the arm became soft and mushy like a ripe tomato. On my next visit, the doctor said the arm was now ready to be lanced.

Our regimental hospital operating room was in a tent with a dirt floor, hardly a place I had envisaged for even a minor operation. I lay down on the operating table, and a corpsman prepared my arm by cleansing it with an antiseptic solution. I was given an anesthetic called sodium pentothal. The doctor asked me to count backward from one hundred on down and I don't remember getting past ninety five before I was off, but I could still hear the doc giving his instructions to the corpsman assisting him. "He will probably be able to feel the scalpel's incision," he remarked to the corpsman assisting him. I sure could, and it felt like a hot poker. I bolted up from the table shouting, "You're damn right! I can feel it, Doc!" He pushed me back down and told me to be quiet so that he could finish the job by letting the poisonous fluid drain. When the doc finished bandaging my arm, I blurted out, "You told me that I would not feel anything, Doc!" Somewhat annoyed, he said that in my anxiety, I fought off the anesthetic. "That's why you felt the incision!" But I was still sore as hell. I was grateful the incision healed well, because the hot steamy climate in these islands usually made wounds take more time to heal. Today, over sixty years later, the scar is still visible from the incision.

After three weeks or so, my arm healed sufficiently, so I volunteered to hitch a ride for the men in our tent to an Army PX. Army post exchanges always had a wide variety of items rarely seen by us in our PX's. I collected a list from the guys in the tent, and I hitched a ride that would cover around fifteen miles each way. Hitching rides on Guadalcanal was never a problem. Any one of the service branches would always pick us up, especially when we wore our camouflage fatigues.

As our jeep passed Carney Airfield, I noticed several B-24s lined up with their engines running, and asked the driver to let me off. I ran across the airstrip. The bomber crews were standing alongside their planes, waiting for the signal to take off. I approached one of the pilots. His shoulder bars indicated that he was a captain. I brazenly asked, "Which target are you guys hitting today?" He looked me over from head to foot, noticed the U.S.M.C. above the left-hand pocket of my camouflage fatigues, and curtly replied, "Our target is probably going to be your next campaign, marine!" "And what island might that be?" "The target we're plastering today is Kavieng, New Ireland." "No kidding?" I replied.

While the air crews waited around, I asked if I could look under the plane's fuselage. I started counting the bombs in their racks. "Are those 500 pounders?" I asked. "Man alive, I counted nine of them!" Impulsively I asked the crew, "Mind if I go along with you guys on the raid?" "Hey, marine, be our guest," the crew answered in unison. "We should be taking off in about five minutes."

As the minutes ticked away, I began to think the better of it. As the crew started climbing aboard, the captain asked, "Well, are you coming or not?" "Hey!" I replied, "If this plane does not return from the raid, my C.O. will have me down as a deserter, and I'm in enough hot water with him already!" "Suit yourself," the captain replied. In a few minutes the twelve bombers taxied onto the runway. As I watched with mixed emotions, I could not help but think of what a fantastic experience I was missing. However, I never found out if all the bombers returned safely.

When I returned to my tent with the goodies I had purchased, I told the men of my experience and how I declined the opportunity to go on the raid. "So you chickened out, huh?" they taunted. I thought that if I had made that flight, what a great experience it might have been. Well, so much for the fortunes of war.

Some time around August or early September, we were fortunate to have a USO tour arrive on Guadalcanal. USO tours usually had many Hollywood actors and entertainers visit the islands. On this particular evening, after one of our scheduled boxing matches, a boxing ring would be used for the USO troop to entertain us. Two of the entertainers were actor Ray Bolger and the accomplished pianist, Little Jack Little. One of the men in the audience asked Mr. Bolger if he was set up to do the same dance routine from the picture *Stage Door Canteen*. He borrowed a jacket from one of the marines in the audience. It was a great evening for all, but as luck would have it, right in the middle of Mr. Bolger's routine, the air-raid sirens went off and all the electric lights were shut down.

Hundreds of men, including myself, made a mad dash for our respective campsites. Because it was pitch-black, I could not see a large hole just ahead of me; luckily I only fell some five or six feet before hitting bottom. That split second before I hit the bottom of the hole seemed like an hour. I scrambled up and made it back to my campsite and into my foxhole to wait out the air raid. The enemy air raid was one of the heaviest so far, with several bombs exploding right across our camp. One large piece of the bomb's fragments came whirring through the air and plopped only a few feet from my foxhole. As I groped in the dark, I touched the jagged edge of hot metal, which caused me to withdraw my hand instantly.

Of all the hikes we made on Guadalcanal, one in particular, above Henderson Airfield, was quite memorable. This particular section of the island is where some of the bitterest fighting took place. In October and November 1942, the enemy made some of their heaviest attacks on our marine units in a vain attempt to retake Henderson Airfield. Marine elements of the First Marine Division in some of the most vicious fighting of the Guadalcanal campaign, beat back over and over again successive night attacks on our marines' thinned-out positions. Although the Japanese units were constantly reinforced, they were unsuccessful; even though our tough marine unit's ranks were weakened from weeks of fighting, we held and prevailed.

As our company hiked through these former battlegrounds, we could still see the half-filled-in dirt foxholes and many trees still showing the scars of battle from the mortar and artillery fire. We also saw remnants of some of our fighter aircraft that were shot down, and one grave we passed had the fighter plane's propeller as its marker for the buried fighter pilot.

Renewal

On Pacific island battlegrounds,
In contrast now serene;
My thoughts return some sixty years,
A wide-eyed young marine.

The jungle's high new canopy,
Artillery once did glean;
Reach toward the sky so passionately,
Now renewed in luscious green.

Remarkably, just how the Earth,
Plays out its vital role;
How Mother Earth now returns,
To God, whom we extol.
—The author

Bougainville

On October 13, 1943, our third and ninth regiments boarded transports off Guadalcanal and proceeded to Efate, New Hebrides. There a complete rehearsal of landing exercises took place in preparation for the Bougainville Campaign. After a week, with all exercises completed, all forces assembled on their way to Bougainville, BSI. On November 1, at approximately seven a.m., the first of our assault troops stormed the beaches. For most of the men, it was their baptism of fire. Our 21st regiment would be held in reserve a few days, while our own third battalion was held in reserve for over a week.

When the third battalion left Guadalcanal for Bougainville, our LST convoy anchored in the Tulagi Island channel and waited for the rest of our convoy to assemble. With nothing else to do but wait, several poker games naturally ensued on the deck, with myself as an eager participant. Well into the poker games, a gust of wind blew most of the paper money from the deck into the channel. It took only a few seconds before several of us stripped down; but being the fastest, I dove over the side of the LST before anyone else.

I swam as fast as I could. I managed to collect several one and five dollar bills, but as I attempted to retrieve more, I heard our sergeant bellow out, "Friedman, get your ass back on deck, *now!*" When I got aboard, the sergeant proceeded to chew my ass out for that "stupid stunt." Nevertheless, I dried out the wet bills and quickly returned to another poker game—but unfortunately lost the money anyway. Well, I simply chalked it up to the fortunes of war. The next day, our convoy assembled and we left Tulagi for our rendezvous with Bougainville.

On the third day, our LST convoy entered Empress Augusta Bay. At three a.m., I was sound asleep on the ship's deck lying between two 20mm AA guns. Unfortunately for me, none of the ship's crew found it convenient to awaken me. Suddenly thunderous blasts from those 20mm guns abruptly woke me up and totally confused me. I hadn't the slightest notion as to what in the hell was going on. As I bolted to my feet, I could see thousands of red tracers from our ship's guns directed at one of the enemy torpedo planes bearing down on us, which was quite visible in the bright moonlight. It took me about twenty seconds to get my bearings from all that confusion.

In less than five minutes, a torpedo struck the destroyer *McKean*, just off to our port side with a full company of marine infantry aboard. About thirty-eight marines lost their lives. When our own LST reached the shoreline around seven a.m., enemy dive-bombers attacked us directly out of the sun, which made them difficult to see, and dropped a few bombs just astern of our ship. This caused giant plumes of water to leap skyward. Although our ship's AA weapons were firing away at the attacking dive-bombers, I did not see any hits on the enemy. Our platoon immediately left the LST and dashed across the beach, taking cover in the dense jungle overgrowth.

It took most of the day for our equipment to get ashore. By evening our platoon dug foxholes on the beach awaiting orders to move inland. Around nine p.m., enemy bombers flew directly over the beach area and dropped several bombs so close to our foxholes that heavy concentrations of sand showered over us. The bombs, which made crunching "harumps" as they exploded near us, were terrifying. One bomb hit a 90mm anti-aircraft gun pit, killing the entire gun crew along with four of our men and leaving six others wounded. By midmorning, our platoon moved inland. We came upon twenty to twenty-five dead enemy soldiers strewn all over the place. Clearly these Jap soldiers were ambushed by units of the Second Raider battalion. Enemy mess gear and rice lay strewn all over the area. No doubt the enemy was ambushed while eating.

Moving inland another five hundred yards, we reached battalion headquarters and dug a perimeter defense around some tents set up as a field hospital. At night a bright lamp was lit in one of the tents, so I peeped inside and momentarily watched two surgeons operating on a wounded marine's leg. Moving out again by morning, we finally set up a temporary bivouac in a lightly wooded area about fifty yards or so from a hill. The next morning, being a little too curious for my own good, I decided to climb up the hundred-foot-high hill, which had a narrow path leading to the top.

Neglecting to inform anyone of my intentions, I started up the narrow winding path. When I reached the top, I could not believe my eyes. There before me was a maze of tunnels crisscrossing one another with connecting trenches. The area was quiet as a graveyard … it seemed as though the enemy had deserted these well-fortified positions. Continuing on my own to inspect this amazing labyrinth of tunnels, I must have been spotted by an enemy forward observer. Like a crack of lightning, two mortar shells struck the top of the tall trees well above me.

Those two mortar bursts scared the living hell out of me, and I must have leaped ten feet through the air into the nearest hole within reach. All alone, I was hunkered down in the deep trench like a scared rabbit. As I lay hidden in the trench, I felt a stinging sensation in my left forearm. Nervously rolling up my sleeve, I could see a raised bluish area that was slightly swollen, with practically no bleeding. As I probed the slight wound with my forefinger, I could feel a solid object imbedded just below the skin line.

I must have waited at least twenty minutes before I felt it would be safe to make my way down the hill. When I returned to my foxhole, I was in a real quandary as to how to explain my predicament. Nervously approaching our corpsman after quietly calling him aside, I showed him my forearm. "How did you get that, Friedman?" he inquired. In hushed tones, I told him what had happened and how I had made my way up the hill, including the shell bursts. Well, he could barely suppress his anger. "You ass, what in the living hell were you doing up there all alone? Come into my tent and let me take a look at it." Using a forceps, he probed the area and pulled out a small piece of metal about the size of a match head.

Applying antiseptic powder, the corpsman bandaged the small wound. While rolling down my sleeve, he quietly remarked, "You know, Friedman, I am going to keep this quiet because you might get a court-martial for that crazy stunt." Thanking him, I agreed that I had no intention of mentioning the incident to anyone.

Moving up to forward positions the next morning, we came upon another enemy position that was abandoned. Rather than dig a new foxhole for the evening, my squad sergeant and I started filling in the foxholes dug by the Japanese. In order to escape our heavy artillery barrages, the enemy foxholes were dug fairly deep. While using my entrenching shovel to partially fill in the enemy foxhole, I sliced a four-foot snake in half and tossed the snake's remains away. The sergeant and I put coconut logs over our foxhole, covering the logs with large banana leaves covered with soil. Even with the daily drenching rains, we felt secure we would stay dry.

About nine p.m., lying side by side, using our steel helmets as pillows, I felt something lightly brush across both my legs about ankle high. Half sitting up while reaching forward, my right hand grabbed a snake. I yelled loud enough to be heard clear across the island. In a split second, I tossed the damn thing out of the foxhole and blurted, "Hey, Sarge, I just tossed out a God damn snake, which had run right across my legs." "I know, I felt him too," he replied. "Thanks a lot for not telling me!" I angrily responded.

Unfortunately, the snake incident does not end yet. That damn snake must have been searching around for its mate, which I had killed earlier with my entrenching shovel. The damn thing crawled back just over our heads among the logs, with small pieces of dirt falling on our heads all night. Had anyone taken a moment to inspect our foxhole with a flashlight, the sergeant and I would have looked like two mummies, frozen in fear. I don't think we even blinked an eye all night long. It occurred to me that the snake might be poisonous. That particular night was probably the longest night in both our memories.

By morning, there was another surprise in store for everyone on the island. Bougainville's 9,000-foot Mt. Bagana, as far as we knew, was the only active volcano in the Solomon Islands. The volcano was easily visible from almost anywhere on the island, except from the deep jungle. Gazing at the volcano, which constantly emitted a column of steam, always left us a little uneasy.

On the morning of November 21 or 22, the ground under us started shaking violently in a rolling action. Wow! Talk about being frightened! We all just froze in our tracks. The shaking and rumbling must have lasted at least thirty seconds, and the hill that

I had climbed the day before was rolling like a large mound of Jell-O. Our frightened faces manifested just how utterly helpless we were during those terrifying thirty seconds, and yet we were to experience another severe jolting some three weeks later.

Around December 15, at five in the morning, we were awakened abruptly by another strong jolt, and this time the dirt from the walls of my foxhole began covering me. My foxhole was not deep enough for me to be buried. Nevertheless, I scrambled out like a rabbit. The fact that it was dark made our predicament even more frightening. However, in my typical frontline sophisticated dialogue, that last five a.m. jolt was some "piss call."

As we continued to move up toward forward areas, we met up in late afternoon with several Marine Raiders. They were opening cases of ammunition and food rations recently dropped to them by parachute. Because it was late afternoon, our platoon leader decided we would dig in for the night. With those raiders close by, we felt pretty good. When my own foxhole was finished, I asked one of the raiders if I could use one of the parachutes lying around to line my muddy foxhole with. Without hesitation he told me to help myself.

I was surprised how large the parachute was, having to fold it at least three times in order for it to fit my foxhole, but it still overlapped by a foot or two. Shortly, one of the Marine Raiders walked over and, noticing how comfortable I looked, asked if he could join me. "This will save me from having to dig my own foxhole," he remarked. I sure as hell didn't mind a Marine Raider for company.

Somehow it never occurred to either of us that the white parachute would become a target for a Jap sniper a short distance away, who started to take pot shots at us. After five or six rounds of sniper fire pinging around our foxhole, the Raider, obviously in a nasty mood, stood up, put on his cartridge belt, grabbed his rifle, and started moving in the direction of the sniper's fire. "Where in the hell are you going?" I shouted. "I'm gonna get me that sombitch," he snarled.

It was never a military secret that anyone who personally met a Marine Raider would know that the hatred they had for the enemy practically bordered on distemper. Raiders were widely known to be absolutely fearless, with extraordinary killer instincts. As I anxiously waited while peering in the last direction I had seen the Raider disappear, I did not have to wait very long before three or four shots rang out. In less than a minute, I spotted the Raider walking toward me. I excitedly stood up to greet him.

"Christ, man! What in the hell happened out there?" I asked. "I told you I would get that little sombitch!" he answered grittily. "That little bastard got me though." "Where?" I hastily asked. Turning around, he showed me a bullet hole in the canteen tied to his cartridge belt. Calmly, we both lay down in our luxuriously lined foxhole and spent a reasonably comfortable night. By morning our unit moved out, and I bid the Marine Raider a fond farewell.

Oh, My, Yes ...
Hidden in a banyan tree,
A sniper tried to ambush me;
His first mistake was move his head,
One well-aimed round and he fell dead.

Unnoticed in another tree,
The one I shot had company;
His rifle cracked and it caught me,
In my rear, unceremoniously.

While laying still upon the ground,
Our corpsman's remark was quite profound;
"Take my advice, the next time around;
Make sure your ass stays underground."
—The author

Snipers

In most of our island campaigns, sniper fire from the enemy was fairly sporadic, keeping our casualties minimal. This was not the case on Iwo Jima. The Fifth Marine Division's Twenty-Eighth Regiment, conquerors of Mt. Suribachi, took very high casualties from a well-entrenched enemy on Hill 362A and the area known as The Gorge in the Northern Sector near Kitano Point.

Two-Legged Spiders

Marines won't find these on a map,
The enemy lurking in a spider trap;
And though one's sight be 20/20,
The enemy stayed hidden, like a sentry.

Those simple holes were no façade,
Stay alert, be on your guard;
Because experience proved without a doubt,
Spider trap snipers can take you out.

Sharp eyes and teamwork was the way,
To stalk those snipers and make them pay;
Making sure the enemy knows the sorrow,
Assuring them there's no tomorrow.
—The author

One of the more insidious techniques occasionally employed by the enemy was the use of spider traps. This ingenious device was no more than a hole dug down to about five feet so that its occupant could stand in it with only his head barely aboveground when he raised its cover.

Covered with tied thin branches, interwoven with leaves and grasses, the well-camouflaged top of the hole was very difficult to detect. When an unsuspecting soldier walked by, the enemy slowly raised the lid, usually firing from behind. The only way one could spot the location of those hidden vipers was from the smoke that emanated from his weapon after it was fired.

The following morning our third platoon was integrated with K company. With two other men, we carried our .30 caliber air-cooled machine gun, along with the tripod and two boxes of ammo. Starting an advance of some five hundred yards, we slogged through a swampy area of jungle that marines up ahead had to literally hack their way through in order to make a clearing for our company to pass. With every swing of their machetes, the men doing the hacking were using profanities one would normally hear in a barroom brawl. Bougainville's jungle, with its impenetrable growth, bottomless mangrove swamps, and crocodile-infested rivers, plus millions of insects, thrived in one of the worst rain forests in the Pacific.

The daily torrents of rain kept us thoroughly drenched, including inside our field shoes, twenty-four hours a day. When our advance halted late each afternoon, we dug in our machine gun, making sure to cut down the dense jungle growth in front of us to give us a clear field of fire. Our lieutenant would make sure our weapons had the proper crossfire so that all our other automatic weapons would overlap each other, which was the norm just in case of enemy nighttime infiltration.

In the morning the jungle is quite cool and very damp; that plus being drenched from lying all night in water-filled foxholes meant we were mean and really miserable. Our feet were wrinkled like prunes, and we developed painful jungle sores around our ankles that made it difficult to walk. A pleasant break for us was to take off our wet socks and put on dry ones, applying the foot powder that we usually carried in our packs to make life just a little more comfortable. But in no time, as we advanced through the swampy jungle, our feet would become soaked again, further worsening our jungle sores.

One of the safety strategies I used during frontline duty was to take our combat telephone wire and string it up in a semicircle about six inches above the ground, from tree to tree about thirty feet or so in front of my foxhole. Then I pulled the wire through the rings of hand grenades I had attached to the trees. This little trick was the added insurance I used just in case the enemy tried to infiltrate in the direction of my machine gun emplacement. Of course, the black combat wire was impossible to see at night; any unsuspecting Jap infiltrator could set off the grenades by tripping his foot on the combat wire, thereby pulling out the grenade's ring.

Every unit always seemed to have its proverbial character, and our platoon certainly wasn't any different. During the night, from our well dug-in positions under the dense jungle canopy, one character in our platoon would yell out at the top of his lungs, his shouts resonating through the nighttime jungle with amazing acoustical qualities, "Japanese eat shit!" or "Tojo eats shit!" What the purpose was for these outbursts all night long was anybody's guess, but I thought it may have been his way of instilling some sort of confidence or self-assurance for himself. I might add, though, it did have a tendency to lift our morale a little. A clever remark from my foxhole buddy after those outbursts was ,"You know, Friedman, what's the damn difference? We're eating those lousy K-rations, aren't we?" "Yeah!" I agreed. "Guess you're right at that!"

The only food we had under these primitive living conditions was "C" and "K" rations carried in our packs. By morning, being soaked from head to foot and chilled, the first thing we wanted was something hot. One of the items we carried in our top pack was a small aluminum gadget only three inches high with three collapsed legs. When its legs were spread open, it would stand up as a tiny stove. In the center was a small depression for a chalky white tablet, about the size of an Alka-Seltzer tablet. When lit, the tablet would burn with a hot blue flame. Setting our canteen cups on this little stove would heat our powdered coffee or a packet of chocolate powder that usually came in either C or K rations.

Along with the coffee or chocolate powder was a can of pork and egg yolks, a can of meat and vegetable stew, or a can of American cheese, which we had to open with a metal key or our issued Kabar knife, which was always so handy. A small packet of cigarettes also came with it; but being a non-smoker, I gave my cigarettes away. On those cool wet mornings, my favorite way for making breakfast was to take the tin of pork and egg yolks and punch a hole in the tin to let out some of the oil. Then I would hold the tin over the little stove until I could hear its contents sizzling. When I timed it right, both sides of the pork and egg yolks were nice and crispy. Along with the hardtack biscuits and black soluble coffee, I really got to enjoy my own cooking. Of course, the men would always shake their heads while they gaped at me as though I was nuts. But I just ignored them.

Thanksgiving Day, November 25, 1943, will always be very memorable for our men. With the Torokina airstrip finished, our aircraft were now operating from it regularly. We frontline marines were not aware of it, but somehow and some way, our navy planes landing at the new fighter strip flew in with fresh turkey with all the trimmings. How they managed this miracle of getting the fresh turkey with all the trimmings up to our frontlines was a morale booster of the first order. To this day, it is impossible for me to describe. I still get slightly choked up thinking of that incredible turkey day for a bunch of half-starved marines.

Our company continued to advance each day with very little resistance. At one point, our units advanced so far that from our new frontline positions, we went over a week with very little food. Parachute drops were falling into enemy lines or hanging up high on the treetops well out of reach. Living on our meager rations day after day, I thought I would try my luck fishing. Taking the hooks and fishing line I had saved all these months, I carefully crept toward the riverbank, in order to avoid being seen by enemy snipers.

Staying very low along the bank, I was unsuccessful finding any worms. But when I pulled up clumps of soil just behind me, I saw stuck to the leaves from the heavy dew, a few small moths. Attaching the moth as bait, I flung the fishing line out into the swiftly moving water as hard as I could because the fishing line wasn't weighted with sinkers. Within seconds, as the moth drifted on top of the swift current, I received a strike. Surprisingly, I had caught a rock bass. In my excitement, I almost called out, "Hey, fellas! Look what I caught!"

Fortunately there were three or more moths still stuck to the wet leaves. I took another one and hooked it, and with the same method, caught a second rock bass. Easily finding a third moth stuck to a wet leaf, I caught my third bass. I must have caught at least two pounds of fish, still fighting to keep my emotions in check at my amazing luck. As the sun was beginning to rise, it was now getting lighter. I thought it best to make my way back to our foxhole positions. When the men in my squad saw the fish, they were astonished.

"Now you guys can't give me a hard time about my fishhooks and fishing line," I exclaimed. While I fried the fish in our mess gear, the expressions on the men's faces were as though we were the cat who ate the canary. In the next few days, our remaining ration situation had dwindled to nothing but soluble coffee. In desperation, I asked my squad sergeant if I could leave the frontlines and work my way back to the beach, about five or six miles away, in order to return with any kind of food I could find for our men.

"Friedman!" my squad sergeant replied, "If you leave the frontlines and get caught, it's going to be your ass!" My earnest response was, "I don't give a good God damn. We are out of chow and I'm going!" "Suit yourself! But if you get caught, remember, I never gave you permission to leave," he said. Even though I realized my mission was of a humanitarian nature, nevertheless, if caught or delayed a day or two, I could have faced a firing squad for desertion.

Any attempt to make one's way back to the beach from our frontlines, a distance of around six miles or more, in reality was practically suicide without any compass, but at this time I couldn't care less. We were out of food, and the prospects of getting any were pretty slim. Using the top section of my pack, I proceeded to tie a hand grenade to each of two shoulder straps. I grabbed my M1 rifle and quietly left the frontlines in the direction of the beach.

After a mile or so of plodding through that green hell, I suddenly came onto a wide dirt road under construction by the Seabees. With at least five more miles to go, I approached the first Seabee. I asked him if any vehicles would be heading toward the beach area. "Sure, marine! One of our trucks will be leaving shortly." *What luck*, I thought to myself, and in the next few minutes, I told the Seabee of our plight and he wished me good luck.

The ride to the beach on the dusty road took only fifteen minutes or so, and I thanked the driver for the hitch. Walking onto the beach, scanning the area, I saw a dozen or more tents that were set up by an army anti-aircraft battalion. Walking into the first tent nearest to me, I found three army personnel standing inside. Staring at me with my filthy tattered camouflaged fatigues, my drawn face, and sunken red eyes, plus a four-week-old beard, they looked at me as though they were seeing an aberration.

Barely audible, and with a weak quivering voice, I quietly asked, "Do you men have any chow for me to bring back to my buddies on the frontlines? I have just made my way back from the frontlines, and we do not have any food." Continuing to stare at me in apparent bewilderment, none of the men offered one word in response to my plea. Desperate, plus angry by their lack of response and without contemplating the consequences, I pulled one of the hand grenades from my pack strap and pulled the pin out. I still made sure to hold the grenade's handle firm, which kept it harmless unless I let the handle fly off.

Well, the sight of the grenade sure did the trick. With their eyes open as wide as saucers, they backed away from me, with the palms of their hands extended toward me and pleading, "OK, marine! We will get you whatever you want!" Keeping two of them as hostages, I told the other to bring back some food. In no time he returned with a five-pound tin of hardtack and a gallon of marmalade jelly. Replacing the grenade's pin, I grabbed the two cans and thanked them. I made sure to disappear as fast as I could into the jungle undergrowth and was lucky enough to catch another ride by truck up to the point where I was originally picked up by the Seabee.

From that point, I made my way back to our frontline position. The platoon greeted me with a reception like a conquering hero; with so many handshakes and backslapping that I was sore. The men, without the slightest hesitation, opened the cans of hardtack and jelly. With our wonderful soluble coffee, we commenced to partake of a hardtack and jelly dinner as though it was gourmet dining.

None of the men in our platoon inquired as to how I obtained the goodies. I certainly had no intention of telling them either. But it wasn't more than a day or two that the rumors around the island were flying thick and fast. Some of the talk in other units was about that crazy marine who had pulled a grenade on some army personnel. When one marine from another outfit mentioned the incident to me, I said, "Yeah, no kidding, that guy must be loco or something!" One other rumor I heard, but could not verify, was that General MacArthur's headquarters put out a directive to find that S.O.B. marine who had dared to pull a grenade on his army personnel. Luckily I had the good sense to keep quiet about the incident, or the army probably would have had me hung.

After being north of the Numa Numa trail in these same positions for close to two weeks, we were finally relieved by another company and set up a temporary bivouac near Piva Village, where we bathed ourselves in the river. Wow! Did that soap and water feel good, especially with some clean fatigues. It just so happened that on our way back, we passed a Seabee campsite. When those great guys saw how dirty and haggard we looked, they graciously offered to feed us in their own field mess hall. It was a well-known fact, those tough Seabees and we marines had the highest respect for each other. Marines were never let down by them. The fighting Seabees would always be there to pull us out of a jam.

Reflections

Those jungle scenes were lovely sites,
Especially in their dappled lights;
Those nightly sounds were eerie too.
With morning mist and heavy dew.

> *The fighting here is tough, you know,*
> *Still better than the cold and snow;*
> *I'll take my chance with heat and rain,*
> *Since cold and snow gives me a pain.*

> *Under all that sweaty, jungle grime,*
> *Our faces aged before their time;*
> *Because if you saw what I have seen,*
> *At the ripe old age of seventeen.*
> —The author

Hellzapoppin Ridge

After three days of relaxation in a rear area (some 300 yards behind our frontlines), our lieutenant teamed me up with one of the men in the fourth platoon, telling us to report with our bazooka and make our way up to Hill 600A. The lieutenant told us that a reconnaissance patrol had met with heavy resistance when the enemy returned at night to reoccupy Hill 600A. Although the Japanese were driven off the hill the day before, they still held their old emplacements on the reverse slope of the hill.

While making our way up the narrow path leading to the top of Hill 600A, we passed by at least a dozen dead marines from the Third Parachute Battalion, recently killed in a fierce firefight with the enemy. As we continued to climb toward the top of the hill, our dive-bombers were attacking enemy positions well below us in a valley. When the air attack subsided, the lieutenant told us that our artillery fire was ineffective because the shells were striking the tops of the trees. "You men move down the slope and take a position in those abandoned foxholes. There is a Jap machine gun nest that is holding up our advance!" Though it was very late in the afternoon, my bazooka buddy and I managed to work our way down from the hill's crest about fifty yards or so and took up a position in one of the abandoned foxholes.

As we both scanned the terrain in front of us, I proceeded to load our bazooka, making sure to tap my buddy, a corporal, on the shoulder. This let him know the weapon was armed and ready for firing. Standing up to take aim at what he felt was an enemy machine gun emplacement, he fired the first round. When he kneeled down, I reloaded the bazooka with a second projectile. Once again he stood up and fired into the same area. We could not possibly know how successful we were, but we did not receive any return fire. From a kneeling position, I threw a hand grenade, but because of the sharp decline, my hand grenade was picked up by the enemy and tossed back at us. Fortunately, it landed on top of the dirt mound that was built up around our foxhole, preventing it from falling in on me. I now forced my helmeted head up against the foxhole wall, and the grenade exploded without harming us.

As it was now starting to get dark, we decided to climb back uphill, with the corporal leading and myself following just behind. I hunched my body very low to remain a small target, but the Jap machine gunner apparently spotted me and fired a burst directly at me. It sounded like a Nambu machine gun because of the weapon's very high rate of fire. Falling flat on my back and breaking my fall with both elbows, I looked skyward and saw red tracers passing directly over me. Fortunately for me, the Jap machine gunner elevated his weapon's sight a little too high. This mistake by the enemy machine gunner saved me from getting cut to pieces.

I crouched much lower this time. As the sky became darker, we both made it to the top of the hill safely. The same lieutenant thanked us and said we could return to our own outfit. When we arrived at our bivouac campsite, Corporal Santana's platoon leader questioned us about our ordeal. It was then that I told his lieutenant how Corporal Santana stood up in full view of the enemy and fired those bazooka rounds, fully exposed to the enemy position. The lieutenant listened attentively when I mentioned his bravery.

When our company returned to Guadalcanal some weeks later, during a company formation, our commanding officer called out for Corporal Santana to step front and center. I don't think anyone in the outfit had any previous knowledge of what was to take place. In front of the entire company, Corporal Santana received a citation and medal for gallantry in action against enemy positions on Hill 600A. It was then that I realized that the information I gave to Santana's lieutenant was the reason for him receiving that well-deserved medal.

The entire company was bubbling with pride for him. Besides, we felt it was refreshing to see an enlisted man receive a medal for a change. All too often, our units would have to stand formation and listen to some silly oratory given for some high-ranking officer receiving a medal for some apparently easy duty performed, such as getting supplies up to the frontlines. Time after time, our company's enlisted men distinguished themselves in action after action without receiving even the slightest recognition.

A day or two before Christmas, our lieutenant called five of us aside and told us the C.O. would be taking us on a three-day reconnaissance patrol behind enemy lines. *Uh-oh!* I thought to myself. *Here we go again!* The purpose of the patrol was to locate the furthest extension of the east-west trail from which the enemy, under a hidden jungle canopy, was bringing in supplies. These supply lines, which could not be observed by our reconnaissance aircraft, had to be located and mapped so the artillery, given the proper coordinates, could bring them under fire.

We left just after dusk, with our C.O. leading the five-man patrol. We traveled very light, with no steel helmets, only a cloth cap. In this way we were sure nothing we wore would give off a metallic sound. While we crossed the wide stony flats on each side of the Torokina River during the night, a large enemy coastal gun many miles away was firing into our frontline positions only a few hundred yards behind us. As our patrol lay on the smooth gravel stones looking up into the black starlit sky, we could hear the enemy shells passing over us with an eerie crackling noise. For every enemy shell falling into our lines, our own artillery would answer round for round.

It was only after the artillery barrage ended that the C.O. would let us continue across the shallow but swift-moving waters of the river. Once on the other side of the wide flats, we disappeared into the dense jungle. We were now in Japanese held lines, and it was impressed on us that stealth would be the watchword. We would be using arm and hand signals only, along with clicking, done by compressing our cheeks against our tongues, to gain attention. With no automatic weapons, it was not our job to engage the enemy, but only to bring back the necessary information about the hidden trail.

Rising very early next morning, from their side of the river, we looked back across the flat expanse that separated us from our own lines. Curiously, we spotted an enemy patrol of six men crossing over into our lines at least three hundred yards from us. It was not in our interest or mission to engage them; any attempt to do so at that distance would have been fruitless anyway. Heading in a westerly direction, while maintaining absolute silence, we advanced deep into enemy lines. The terrain on this side of the river wasn't too swampy, but the insects were ferocious and eating us alive. When we took a ration break, we doused ourselves with iodine on our painful insect bites while our C.O. took new coordinates with his compass.

We must have covered close to 750 yards the first day. It was uneventful up to this point, but a little scary nonetheless. Somehow, our own artillery never got the word about our patrol, because several rounds from our own 105mm artillery guns exploded not very far from us. After taking cover under a large tree for the night, we ate our sumptuous K-rations while continuing at the same time to douse ourselves with iodine. In that pitch-black night under a large tree, we chatted away quietly with our C.O. about ourselves. This informality, between our company commander and us enlisted men, was a welcome break from the stark reality of our mission. The night passed without incident.

The second day started out quietly enough. We had now penetrated around 1200 yards behind Japanese lines. By midmorning, the sky opened up with the heaviest of downpours. But the heavy rain did not deter us from moving forward. It's amazing how those large raindrops made such a thunderous noise as they hit the forest's broad-leaved plants and trees. At this point, I happened to be about ten yards in front as point man, cautiously inching my way, when I ran smack into an enemy soldier only thirty feet directly in front of me. With his back toward me, he was bending over what looked to me like the heavy Hotchkiss machine gun, mounted on its tripod. Fortunately for us, he was covering it with large banana leaves in an attempt to keep it dry.

Obviously, the heavy downpour and the ensuing noise it made on the leaves saved my ass and probably the men behind me. Quickly dropping to the ground, I motioned to the men to do likewise. The major crawled up, whispering, "What's up, Friedman?" I pointed to the Jap still covering his weapon. The C.O. whispered, "We will withdraw; remain here and cover our withdrawal." Still lying in the prone position with my rifle's sight on the Jap, I kept on looking down at my rifle's chamber with all the heavy rain pouring from my cloth cap onto the weapon. I could not help thinking to myself, *I sure hope this weapon functions if I have to fire it.*

When I looked back only ten or fifteen seconds later to see where the patrol was, they had completely vanished into the jungle. "Christ," I muttered to myself, *where in the hell did they disappear, and at what point did the patrol enter the jungle?* Running backward with my rifle still pointing in the direction of the enemy, I half panicked, and ran smack into the last man in the patrol, actually knocking him down. Fortunately, it was the platoon sergeant and not the major. But he still chewed me out through gritted teeth in subdued tones, "God damn it, Friedman, what the f—k is wrong with you?"

Scared half out of my wits, all I could do was stammer incoherently. "Sa-sa-sarg, I lo-lo-lost si-sight of you guys." As an afterthought, I felt damn lucky it wasn't our C.O. I ran into, or I'd be back in the doghouse for good. We were now moving out a little faster so as to put some distance from the enemy. After a few hundred yards, our patrol sat under a large tree and the major studied his map. Turning to the sergeant, he said, "You and Friedman set out together on this compass heading and try to pick up that damn trail."

Damn it to hell, anyway, I thought to myself, *I might be getting paranoid, but why in hell does he always seem to single me out for every stinking shit detail?* Anyway, off the sergeant and I went, compass and all, taking the necessary readings so we would be able to return to the same spot under the large tree. Leading the way with the sarge right behind me a few steps, I could not help but continue to grumble to myself. *God, what an eerie feeling roaming through this hellish green jungle, practically alone. Will I ever get through this miserable ordeal in one piece?*

Within five minutes, we came onto a jungle trail. On the other side, about a hundred feet away, were those tree vines that were connected from tree to tree in a wide circle. As I kneeled down and peered ahead, the terrain did not have the heavy jungle growth; it was more like a forest. Suspecting an enemy bivouac encampment, I motioned for the sarge to approach me. Kneeling beside me he asked, "What's up?" "Check these vines. Notice how they circle all the way around." "Did you see anything?" "No, but I thought I heard something like a metallic sound up ahead." As we both listened for some type of noise, there appeared to be some kind of activity up ahead, but the heavy growth obscured our vision. "Let's get the hell out of here!" the sarge said, and I could not be in more agreement.

Using the compass for our return, we moved out at a faster pace, and before we realized it, we came upon our patrol still resting under that large tree. I could see the C.O.'s face. He looked slightly agitated by our sudden appearance, but did not say anything. "Did you find any trail up ahead?" he asked. The sergeant told the C.O. what we had seen, and the C.O. said, "Okay, let's move out and start heading back." That was the best news, and we all willingly followed his order.

Continuing in the direction of the Torokina River, we stopped for the night under a well-foliaged tree and broke out our rations while dousing our arms and necks with iodine that hopefully would give us some relief from those insect bites that now covered half our bodies. We were now in view of that large expanse of the Torokina River area where we originally crossed from our frontlines two days before. We were a lot more relaxed, and our quiet conversation with the C.O. during the night touched on some of our personal thoughts and civilian background. The major seemed like just one of the boys, which was a welcome change that helped break up the tension of the past few days.

By early morning we crossed the wide-open expanse. When we reached our own frontlines, five or six marines from another outfit came out of the jungle and challenged us, but the C.O. straightened them out. When we finally returned to our own bivouac encampment, the men were keenly interested in our three-day adventure. Our C.O. had a large handlebar mustache, which had a tendency to reflect his mood. Each time he would pass by me in our camp area, I thought I detected a wry smile under that large handlebar mustache of his. I could not help thinking, *hey, maybe the guy appreciates me after all.*

January 1, 1944, was only a few day off. Being the last outfit to arrive on Bougainville back in November, we were finally relieved by the Army's 182nd Infantry Regiment. They moved into our frontline positions, taking over our weapons. As our company marched toward the beach area, about seven miles away, we were walking down the road the Seabees built in our honor called Marine Drive. A large sign on the road read: "So when we reach the Isle of Japan, with our caps at a jaunty tilt, we will enter the city of Tokyo, on roads that the Seabees built!" The Third Marine Division and the Second Marine Raider Battalion had signed at the bottom.

Approximately one mile from the beach, our company moved into the heavy jungle growth about fifty yards in from the road for the night. We were to board ship the next day for Guadalcanal. Around eleven p.m., we were awakened by a lone enemy plane that kept circling right over our area at a very low altitude. It sure aroused our curiosity as to why it kept circling so low. We knew the airstrip was only a short distance away, and we peered through the jungle trying to get a glimpse in the direction of the engine's sound. Although it was too dark for that possibility, we suddenly heard two metallic sounding clicks that could not be much more than five hundred feet overhead. Instantly, two very loud swishes were made by the two bombs, which exploded only seventy-five yards or so from us. We all figured that the metallic clicks were from the plane's bomb racks when the two bombs were released.

When we had only a short distance to march before reaching the beach, an army truck convoy, loaded with GI's probably moving up to forward areas, passed our unit as we straddled both sides of Marine Drive. The interservice rivalry that exists between marines and the army was widely known. We marines referred to army personnel as "dogfaces," so when the truck convoy rolled past us, all of our men started barking and howling just to get their goat. In spite of the loud howling by our men, we could hear one of the army dogfaces bellow at the top of his lungs, "Bark, you sons of bitches, you live like dogs!" Standing alongside me, my buddy remarked, "You know, Friedman, that dogface may have something there!"

Only a mile or so from the beach, we boarded landing craft that took us to a waiting transport ship. My painful jungle sores made climbing up those cargo nets very difficult. I immediately reported to the ship's sick bay, where a navy corpsman soaked my feet in an antiseptic solution. Taking a soft brush, the corpsman broke open the pus sores around my ankles. This helped to take away some of the throbbing pain. Adding a heavy coat of zinc ointment, he wrapped both my ankles with gauze. Three days later, on January 8, we arrived back on Guadalcanal. Surprisingly, those jungle sores along with most of the throbbing pain had dissipated.

Ballad of Private Rodger Young

In justifiable tribute every marine sincerely wants to pay high honor to our army combat brethren. We strongly feel it would be a shortcoming on our part to not pay a well-deserved tribute to their line companies, with whom we fought side by side in so many island campaigns. It is with a deep sense of pride to our army comrades in arms that each marine offers with the deepest humility the "Ballad of Private Rodger Young."

Private Rodger Young was killed in action on New Georgia in July 1943. The New Georgia island chain is approximately 125 miles north of Guadalcanal and was mostly an all-army campaign, except for some marine unit participation at Bairoko Harbor. Fighting against a very well-entrenched enemy, Private Rodger Young received our country's highest decoration—the Congressional Medal of Honor for conspicuous gallantry in action. Marines are very proud to claim that army valor and courage alongside our own units was conspicuous, and every marine feels honored by giving the army its well-deserved recognition.

Oh we have no time for glory in the infantry,
And we have no use for praises loudly sung;
But, in every soldier's heart in all the infantry,
Shines the name, shines the name of Rodger Young.
Shines the name, Rodger Young,
Fought and died for the men he marched among;
To the everlasting glory of the infantry,
Lives the story of Private Rodger Young.

Caught in ambush lay a company of riflemen,
Just grenades against machine guns in the gloom,
Caught in ambush 'til this one of twenty riflemen,
Volunteered, volunteered to meet his doom.

It was he who drew the fire of the enemy,
That a company of men might live to fight,
And before the deadly fire of the enemy,
Stood the man, stood the man we hail tonight.

Stood the man, Rodger Young, fought and died
For the men he marched among
To the everlasting glory of the infantry,
Lives the glory of Private Rodger Young.

On the island of New Georgia in the Solomons,
Stands a simple wooden cross alone to tell,
That beneath the silent coral of the Solomons,
Sleeps a man; sleeps a man remembered well.

Sleeps a man, Rodger Young, fought and died
For the men he marched among,
To the everlasting spirit of the infantry
Lives the spirit of Private Rodger Young.
—Frank Loesser

Our return to Guadalcanal and Coconut Grove was welcomed by all. We were given ten days R&R along with our daily showers and a complete set of fatigues, field shoes, and underwear (skivvies), along with a ration of bottled beer; we felt as though we were on vacation. With the run of the island for the next ten days, I was now looking for something a little more exciting. I soon found it.

Our campsite had a small rectangular tent used as our company library. The paraphernalia included a few books, our hometown newspapers, and some magazines. Casually leafing through each magazine, I came across a recent copy of *Life*. I was surprised to see a two- or three-page pictorial display showing many combat photos of the Bougainville campaign, including some very vivid battle scenes along with the enemy dead.

With only a few days left of my R&R, I decided out of curiosity and boredom to visit a Japanese POW camp only ten miles or so north of us. Making sure to take the *Life* magazine with me, I hitched a ride and located the POW compound easily. Peering through the barbed wire surrounding the compound, I could see dozens of enemy prisoners quietly milling around inside.

Looking through the fence, I could see five or six prisoners sitting on a raised wooden floor lazily shooting the breeze. In order to get their attention, I yelled out in my limited Japanese vocabulary, "Who is in charge there?" Looking very surprised as they turned toward me, and apparently astonished at my broken Japanese, one of the prisoners decided to leave the group and slowly walked over to me.

I was surprised to hear him greet me in English. He appeared to be in his mid-twenties. The first question I asked him was where he was captured. He told me he was a fighter pilot and was shot down over Rendova (one of the islands in the New Georgia group). What really annoyed me was his cocky attitude, along with his taunting of the damage done in the attack at Pearl Harbor. Not one to let him get away with that crap, I immediately struck back with my own verbal assault about their own losses at Midway, Guadalcanal, New Georgia, and now Bougainville.

Opening the *Life* magazine, I turned to the pages showing the photos of battle scene skirmishes, including the photo of the enemy dead. Dripping with sarcasm, I remarked, "These are some of your buddies." Well, those photos shut him up, and the gratification I felt was worth a million bucks. Unfortunately, an army officer approached me and asked that I not engage in any conversation with the prisoner. I left the Jap prisoner with a parting verbal salvo, along with the satisfaction that I had the good sense to bring the *Life* magazine along. I could not help but think over and over again how I could not have planned it any better to shove it down his honorable throat.

Back at camp, I heard that some of the Army's 37th Division was back on Guadalcanal, corroborated in a letter received from the family. With my first cousin serving in the 112th Medical Battalion of that division, I hitched a ride and found his unit at least fifteen miles from our camp. Even though some men in my cousin's outfit looked for him, he was nowhere to be found. They also informed me that his jeep was gone, so I returned to camp pretty disappointed. Entering my tent with my head down, I was pleasantly surprised when I heard that familiar voice out of the past … yes, it was none other than my cousin.

With his own personal jeep, we drove back to his camp, where he introduced me to his army friends. Since I had recently returned from Bougainville, his army buddies were quite interested in some of my action experiences. My cousin not only had the luxury of his own jeep but also owned a camera, and we took several photos together. It's hard to describe what it meant to see a close member of the family thousands of miles from home. Having arrived in Australia in the summer of 1942, he mentioned that he was soon to be rotated back to the U.S.A. About six weeks later, I saw him board a transport off Lunga Point for his return home.

With our new heavy training schedule in tank-infantry tactics and assaults on fortified positions, our exercises soon overshadowed that depressed feeling at my cousin's recent departure to the states. By late March 1944, with our training over, all units of our Third Marine Division were fully combat loaded aboard troop transports anchored off Guadalcanal in preparation for our next campaign, Kavieng, New Ireland. Our navy's high command was in contact with General MacArthur, whose army forces had made landings in the Admiralty Islands. These islands dominated the entire archipelago, which made it unnecessary for our own Third Marine Division to land at Kavieng; thus the entire division disembarked and went back to Coconut Grove to set up camp once more.

Our training preparation for the Kavieng operation had keyed all units in the division to a very high pitch, causing a slight letdown by the new orders. In order to raise the level of our morale, several parades were conducted during the month of April. The first parade carried out was with our individual weapons, but our second parade included all of the regiment's weapons and was reviewed by the corps commander, along with other top-ranking marine and navy officers.

Camp Lejeune, North Carolina, October 1942.

Training photos, San Diego, California, December 1942.

Training photos, San Diego, California, December 1942.

On Guadalcanal, April 1944, Gun Squad (author
pictured in top row, second from right).

Guadalcanal, February 1944, with my cousin.

Top and bottom photos, taken by combat photographer, show the author helping wounded down from Fonte Ridge on the first day of the Guam campaign. Tramways were constructed to evacuate the wounded from the crest.

On leave from Iwo Jima (June 1945).

Our enemy—two Japanese soldiers.

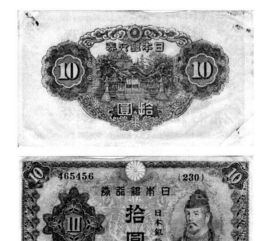

Japanese 10 yen (front and back) taken from
the enemy, Iwo Jima, March 1945.

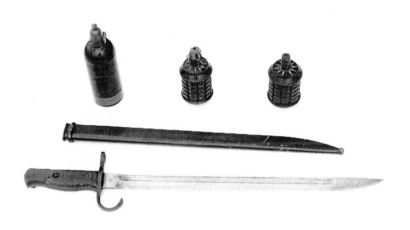

This 50mm enemy mortar shell and the two Japanese grenades were retrieved from enemy positions on Iwo Jima and disarmed there by the author. Although our grenades were larger and a little heavier, enemy hand grenades had a more powerful blast. The use of picric acid in their grenades probably accounts for this. The Japanese bayonet was taken from the enemy on Guam. A bullet crease on the scabbard is barely noticeable due to the size of the photo.

Return to Guam, July 16–22, 1994. Landing site and
dedication memorial to those who led combat patrols
on Guam during September to November 1944.

The author's dog tags.

Guam

Guam, the largest and southernmost island in the Marianas, is an unincorporated territory of the United States. Located 1,400 miles east of the Philippine Islands, it was an important military base even before World War II. About thirty miles long and some four to eight miles wide, it contains 209 square miles. Guam's population today is approximately 200,000 people.

Known today as Guamanians, the indigenous inhabitants were the Chamoros, with their own distinctive language and culture, a mixture of European and Oriental strains, among which Spanish and Filipino are dominant. Although English is the official language, a Chamoro dialect is still spoken. Rebuilt heavily after World War II, its capital of Agana has attractive modern buildings and wide paved streets. The land is volcanic in origin and rises steeply from the world's greatest known ocean depths.

Guam's economic mainstays are U.S. military installations, with Anderson Air Force Base as a major defense installation and Marine and Coast Guard units also stationed on Guam. Although its people are U.S. citizens, they may not vote in our national elections and are not represented in the U.S. Congress. Taken out of jurisdiction of the U.S. Navy, a civilian administration was established under the Department of the Interior.

The Marianas Islands were discovered by Ferdinand Magellan in 1521. Spain took possession of Guam in 1565. Spanish missionaries arrived in 1688 and converted the people to Christianity. Finally ceded by Spain to the United States by the Treaty of Paris at the end of the Spanish-American War in 1898, Guam became a base for the U.S. Navy.

Guam was the first American territory occupied by the Japanese shortly after Pearl Harbor and was the first American territory to be recaptured by our forces, in August 1944. By early May 1944, operational plans were made for the Third Marine Division to coordinate landings on Saipan with the Second and Fourth Marine Divisions. Leaving Guadalcanal late May for practice landings, we then embarked on LST's. Our Third Battalion, Twenty-First Regiment, was designated as the assault troops at Asan Beach for the Guam campaign. Arriving in Kwajalein Harbor, Marshal Islands, in the first week of June, we left shortly to augment as floating reserve for the Saipan landing.

On our way to the Saipan invasion, our LST's navy gunnery officer asked if any of us aboard were familiar with the .50 caliber machine guns. I immediately volunteered. "Go down into the ship's hold and take out any .50 caliber you see and mount it on any one of the gun mounts here on deck," he told me. Carrying the machine gun up from the hold was difficult, especially with the heavy oil coating I needed to remove, but I was given enough kerosene to do a thorough cleaning job. After setting the shiny, clean weapon on its gun mount, I was provided with plenty of .50 caliber ammunition and proceeded to cover the weapon with a canvas cover for its protection.

Being the only marine aboard ship to volunteer for the job, at least I had the opportunity to fire it along with the navy personnel at target practice. Besides, it offered me something to do other than languishing on deck playing cards hour after hour.

On our way toward Saipan, around five p.m. while we stood on the chow line, the ship's warning system sounded. Racing at top speed along with many of the ship's crew to general quarters, I immediately pulled off the weapon's canvas cover and half loaded the weapon, making my .50 caliber weapon ready for action. And action would be immediately forthcoming, because as I looked out toward starboard, I could see the first two of five Japanese torpedo planes already bearing down on us about one-half mile out.

As the first enemy torpedo bomber started making its run at us, the gunnery officer over the PA system instructed the 40mm gun crews to open fire first because of their longer range. The 20mm weapons were next. My .50 caliber fired last because of its shorter range. One of the 40mm gun turrets was about ten feet above my head, and when that double-mounted weapon started firing, the deafening blasts from its muzzle practically drove me crazy. With the enemy torpedo plane now closing in so fast, I just ignored the fierce concussion.

When the first Japanese plane came within range, I opened fire. Having led the target perfectly, I could see my tracers pouring into the cowling of the torpedo plane's engine as it crossed over the bow of our LST, attempting to climb. Within seconds, the torpedo plane exploded as it raced across the front end of our ship. At a height less than two hundred feet, it showered pieces that fell dangerously close to us. It's a wonder that the falling debris did not mince the men on deck.

There was no time to cheer because just behind it a second torpedo plane was making its run at us. When it came within range, I commenced firing and made sure to lead it enough so that my tracers would hopefully find their mark. Along with all the other ship's AA firing, I could see my own tracers plowing into the enemy plane's engine. Again, as the enemy plane crossed our ship's bow, it caught fire, and about a half mile away, it crashed into the ocean.

As the third torpedo plane approached, it dropped its torpedo, which struck the LCI just two hundred yards to our port side, slightly forward of our LST. About forty feet of the ship's bow was sheared off, and fortunately, the tons of ammunition it carried did not explode—it was close enough to us to have probably caused many casualties on our own LST. However, seventeen men aboard the LCI lost their lives, and we helped pick up several survivors. It was later sunk by one of our destroyers when the rest of the ship continued to stay afloat. I was anxious to see how many rounds of .50 caliber ammo I had fired. A quick check of my ammunition box showed that I had expended about ninety rounds at the three enemy planes.

Unnoticed by myself during that entire melee, a combat photographer happened to be standing just behind me and had been taking pictures. "Do you mean to say, sir, that while all that firing was going on, you were taking pictures of the entire action?" I asked him after things settled down. "I sure did, and I could see you did some fancy shooting also." "Say, just what do you do with those pictures you have taken of the attack?" I asked. "Well, these will go immediately to intelligence for evaluation; our navy wants to know just what type of aircraft the enemy is using against us."

My conversation with the combat photographer was interrupted by a group of sailors about thirty feet to my left. One of them was shouting obscenities that could be heard all over the ship. Curious to see what the shouting was all about, I walked over and noticed that about two feet of this sailor's

20mm gun barrel had been shot off. He was fit to be tied! It immediately occurred to me that I must have been the culprit. In my exuberance during the firing, I most likely traversed my weapon practically parallel to the ship's deck in order to get those last rounds off at the disappearing enemy bomber. I thought it best to just let sleeping dogs lie and not admit my probable guilt. This sailor was so pissed, he probably would have tossed me over the side of the ship.

But my mistake was trivial compared to what was soon to take place. On the opposite side of our convoy, one of our own navy torpedo bombers was flying parallel to our convoy no more than fifty feet high. Some trigger-happy gun crew, still jittery from the enemy attack an hour before, shot our plane down with its first burst. The gunnery officer over our ship's PA system was outraged as he announced, "That was a navy TBF that was shot down." Of course, I heard there was hell to pay for that stupidity, because navy gun crews are given adequate schooling in enemy aircraft identification.

Next day I was given KP duty and was in a great position to give my own men some extra food while serving on the chow line. Besides that, I would take a loaf of bread after dinner and tuck it under my shirt. When none of the ship's crew was watching, I would sneak down below to the ship's commissary room and pilfer those large cans of boned chicken. Sometime around nine or ten in the evening, we would cautiously make chicken sandwiches on that loaf of bread that I pilfered. The men in my platoon undoubtedly were the best-fed marines aboard ship.

Another side benefit of KP duty was the bunk bed I was offered belowdecks. Now I would not have to sleep alongside those trucks with our attached pup-tent lean-tos during all those rain squalls we always ran in and out, which kept us drenched half of the time. Another bonus the bunk bed gave was I could stock my pack, rifle, and other items in what I thought would be a safe haven. After serving the men on the chow line, I returned to my bunk bed and noticed my rifle was missing. I immediately reported the theft to our lieutenant, and both of us went to the ship's captain to report my missing weapon.

With the landing only a few days away, I could hardly restrain my anger. I actually started to chew out the ship's captain about the kind of men on ship that would steal a man's weapon. My lieutenant kept on grabbing my arm in order to quiet me down, but I was in no mood to do so. Finally the captain asked me to relax. "We will make a thorough check of all the lockers of this ship's crew." It took about a half-hour, and the weapon was finally found in one sailor's locker. I still found it difficult to forgive this unconscionable deed.

In order to avoid a repetition of the theft, I decided to take revenge on the ship's crew that would have a lasting effect. I took two hand grenades from my pack, and I tied each of them to the steel posts that held the bunk beds secure. Of course, I made sure that the grenade's pins remained firmly secured. Well, when those sailors passed by my bunk bed and saw those two hand grenades attached, they gave my bunk a ten-foot-wide berth. Finally the ship's chief petty officer approached me and asked, "Please, would you take those grenades off. The men are very frightened of them." "If you can prevent another repetition of someone stealing my rifle, I'd be happy to comply with your request, chief," I replied. And with that, our mutual agreement was sealed.

On June 15, 1944, the Second Marine Division and Fourth Marine Division assaulted the beaches of Saipan, while our Third Marine Division stood well offshore in reserve. The navy top brass decided to postpone our landing because ships and aircraft to support us for the Guam landing could not be spared. Besides, a great fleet action was about to take place in the now-famous battle of the Philippine Sea. The navy's high command thought it prudent to protect our division on troop transport ships from exposure to the enemy's surface action in trying to thwart the Saipan landing. We were therefore ordered back to Eniwetok Harbor in the Marshall Islands and out of harm's way.

Our entire Third Marine Division waited for over two weeks for the preparatory sea and air bombardment of Guam's airfields and shore defenses in a softening-up measure that would make our landing less hazardous. About July 14, our LST convoy left Eniwetok Harbor. The main body of transports followed about fifty miles behind our LST convoy.

An unusual incident occurred on our third day out. About eleven p.m., many of us were casually gazing from the deck of our LST in the night's blackness, when off in the distance a bright glare illuminated the sky. As this bright glare drew closer, we could see a large red cross on the side of the large ship, which identified it as one of our own hospital ships. Because our own convoy was completely blacked out, the hospital ship obviously could not see our convoy and it came perilously close to us. It abruptly changed course and was out of harm's way.

Before dawn, just a few hours before H-hour, many of us stood along the ship's rail watching the flashes from our Navy's heavy guns bombarding Guam's coastline. Although we must have been thirty miles away, the report from those big navy guns could easily be heard. Standing next to me on deck was our company warrant officer, and I remember asking just how difficult a landing could be expected. Although we were offered breakfast, I declined it. With my stomach doing flip-flops, the last thing I wanted was food.

At the crack of dawn on July 21, our LST convoy stood about two miles off Guam's coastline. Not very far from our stationary ships we could see two battleships, cruisers, and destroyers bombarding the shoreline, while simultaneously our dive-bombers dove on their assigned targets in a dazzling display of firepower. The entire beach area was covered with heavy smoke that had our men inwardly cheering as each bomb and shell crashed on shore.

Our own Third Battalion, Twenty-First Regiment was scheduled to land at eight thirty a.m. By seven thirty, we were already in our landing craft belowdecks awaiting orders to disembark. When all our landing crafts' engines started up, the exhaust from them was stifling and one could hardly see twenty feet. When our steel doors finally opened, we received some relief. By eight a.m., all of our men on the landing craft disembarked safely down that steep ramp, fortunately into a fairly calm sea. We were now very close to one of our battleships firing broadside after broadside, and what an awesome sight it was. One could actually see their 14-inch shells as they flew toward the beach while our landing craft continuously circled round and round, waiting for the order to go in.

Finally, around eight thirty, an amber-colored flare exploded high above the shoreline. This was the signal for all assault wave units to head toward the beach. We must have been just a little over a mile from shore when the enemy's mortar and artillery started crashing around all our landing crafts as they raced toward the shoreline. While our men crouched down, I happened to take notice of a stack of artillery shells at the rear of our craft. "Hey, you guys, do you see what the hell we are carrying?" With so many mortar and artillery shells crashing around us, I made the decision to jump off our landing craft as soon as we reached the coral shelf.

Jumping off in water that was only four feet deep, approximately two hundred yards from shore, I noticed that all of the men in our landing craft had also jumped off and were wading ashore just behind me. With the mortar fire crashing all around us, I thought we all had a better chance to survive by abandoning the landing craft. Making shore safely, I turned around to see how many men had followed me in. Within seconds, the landing craft we had deserted took a direct hit, and all I could see was a big ball of orange flames.

Racing inland with artillery fire exploding around us, I came upon a large rectangular pit some fifty feet long and twenty feet wide, filled with at least thirty or more marines taking cover from that merciless artillery fire. Sensing that the large tank trap could be a magnet, I decided not to take cover there. I crawled to the nearest palm tree that had been sheared off by our own shoreline bombardment and took temporary cover until the mortar fire subsided.

With my steel helmet shoved against the coconut tree, it was only a minute or so before a mortar shell burst directly into that large tank trap. The screams from the wounded men in the tank trap were absolutely frightful. Crawling over to help, I started pulling out the wounded and some that did not make it. Shortly, some of our corpsmen arrived. When most of the heavy fire subsided, I moved inland another hundred yards and found a ready-made foxhole. I leaped into it for cover.

Without my realizing it, only thirty feet from me were several men from my platoon in their own foxhole. A minute or so later, I heard our lieutenant call to me, "Hey, Friedman, c'mon over and pick up some candy bars!" Although I was reluctant to leave the safety of my foxhole, I had only thirty feet to that candy and decided to risk it. Scrambling out as fast as I could, I grabbed the candy bars from the lieutenant's outstretched hand without saying a word and ran back, actually leaping through the air right into my own foxhole in one big jump.

Within seconds, three mortar shells exploded inside the lieutenant's foxhole, either killing or wounding all of the men in it. Screaming for our corpsmen, we pulled out the wounded and dying while rendering assistance. I remember turning to our head corpsman, asking him how badly the lieutenant was hit. He said he had a massive wound in the spinal area and doubted if the lieutenant would last five more minutes. Pleading with the corpsman, I said, "Let's get him to the beach area and out to the hospital ship." "It's no use, Friedman—the lieutenant's wound is so massive he cannot survive." No matter how I pleaded, I was told it was useless. As I kneeled down alongside this fine sensitive man, he passed away before my very eyes.

OUR NAVY CORPSMEN

What are those men in jungle greens,
Attending wounds on our marines;
Conspicuous loyalty throughout the war,
Fighting beside us within our Corps,
What greater tribute can we now give,
Than honor them while we still live.
—The author

"Corpsman! Corpsman!" … Can any marine forget the many agonizing cries of our wounded during fierce skirmishes and the selfless devotion to duty by our navy corpsmen while attending to our wounded under fire? We marines acknowledge a sacred duty by giving credit where credit is due. We salute all the valiant, dedicated corpsmen who served with our marine units— they were in the very best traditions of the U.S. Navy.

One of our men carried his wounded buddy the hundred yards or so to a beach aid station. Part of his hand was blown off, and he had a puncture wound in his lung. Taking a look at him, the doctor said that he could not survive. He also would not permit his pal to board a landing craft with other wounded to take him to the hospital ship lying offshore. Pulling his .45 automatic pistol from his holster and pointing the weapon at the doctor's head, our man threatened to shoot him unless he put his buddy aboard the landing craft. Interestingly, it was that personal action that actually saved his buddy's life, because once aboard the hospital ship, he received medical attention, which ultimately pulled him through.

Most of our company was ashore now, and our C.O. had us set up a perimeter defense around a battery of 105mm Howitzers, which had already been set up as support fire for our line companies now engaging enemy forces on Fonte Ridge about a thousand yards forward of us. By midafternoon, our C.O. ordered three men and myself up to Fonte Ridge to help bring down some of our wounded men. We helped put the wounded men on stretchers. The stretchers were attached to steel cables that ran from the top of Fonte Ridge down a very steep slope. Once lowered, the wounded were taken to a temporary field hospital or aboard the hospital ship.

When I reached the top of Fonte Ridge, I noticed the same combat photographer who was aboard our LST taking pictures of the torpedo attack. When I asked him if he remembered me, he acknowledged that he did. When I was halfway down the steep slope, helping lower our wounded, he took pictures of me. The photos of me were in our Third Marine Division book given to every member of our division after the war.

On my way back to our company, I came across several marines standing around a captured Japanese soldier who had three bullets embedded in the calf of his leg. The same doctor who lanced my arm on Guadalcanal casually proceeded to take out each bullet with his forceps. All the Jap did was wince a little in spite of not being given any anesthesia.

On the night of July 25, the enemy made several fierce probing attacks at several of our positions along the Chonito Hills, but all units steadfastly repulsed every attack. Around ten p.m., our C.O. ordered our third platoon up to Fonte Hill's right flank. Clawing our way in total darkness up the steep slope, we finally made it, half stumbling over many marines already dug in there. Some enemy probing attacks were made around one a.m. but were broken up by our mortar fire. Around five a.m., under a heavy mortar barrage, all living hell broke loose along our entire frontline positions. Approximately four thousand enemy troops came over the ridge screaming in unison, "Banzai," with their officers leading this full-scale frontal assault, brandishing and waving their samurai swords.

Directly in front of my foxhole position, only fifty to sixty yards away, hundreds of enemy troops were charging us in a direct assault on our foxhole positions. My instant thought was, *Christ, Joe, you're a dead man.* Fortunately for us, an unbroken barrage of illuminating parachute flares from our artillery positions lit up the frontlines as though it was daylight. I began firing my M1 from the prone position from my shallow foxhole, directly into the masses of enemy troops bearing down on us.

Firing at the enemy as fast as I could, I made sure to aim directly at the midsection of their bodies for what I felt had the best killing effect. With eight rounds in each clip, I must have fired at least four clips before the Japs reached our foxhole positions. Instead of engaging us in hand-to-hand fighting, they leaped over our foxholes in order to get behind our positions to knock out our mortar and artillery units behind the frontlines.

With our frontline positions brightly lit, I could see some hundred yards to our left several enemy soldiers clambering over two of our tanks, attempting to get the tanks' hatches open. As I swung my M1 around, I sighted in on the enemy, who were still trying to get the hatches open. But as I glanced just ahead of me, the Japs were still coming straight at our positions. I was forced to change my focus onto the masses of enemy troops just ahead. Thank God for those parachute flares because they gave us a fighting chance.

Enemy Banzai Charge
Guam, July 26, 1944, 5 am–8 am

Along the length of Fonte Ridge
Four thousand Japanese charged;
Racing down the hill towards us,
Behind a mortar barrage.

With frightful yells and fearful rage,
The enemy screamed "banzai";
Keep up that steady fire, men,
Or surely we will die.

Hitting us from every side,
Our sergeant clearly yelled;
"Fix your bayonets, men,
Let's send them all to hell."

When daylight came to greet us,
We grimly looked around;
Hundreds of the enemy,
Lay still upon the ground.

But we always will remember,
With the enemy's final charge;
Those frightful screams of banzai,
Behind their mortar barrage.
—The author

Just to my left, I could see some of our men using their .45 automatics as the enemy leaped over their foxholes. Suddenly, I heard the sergeant in the foxhole twenty feet to my left yell out, "Fix your bayonets, men!" "Hell," I muttered to myself, *I'm not wasting time reaching for my bayonet when the Japs are this damn close!* I quickly took notice that all the marines dug in all around my own position were steadfastly holding their positions without giving up an inch of ground. *God almighty,* I thought to myself, *what marines!* Every man was pouring deadly rifle and automatic weapon fire into the attacking enemy. We had the enemy dead and wounded stacked up inches from our individual foxholes.

By the first light of dawn, the fierce enemy attack had spent itself. The carnage, with enemy dead and wounded all around us, was unbelievable. It was then that we were able to carry our own wounded down the steep slopes just behind us. Unfortunately, as we were milling around the top of the ridge attending the wounded, our own artillery men from the beach area must have thought we were the enemy. They fired a salvo of four 75mm shells that crashed right on top of us while we were putting our wounded on stretchers; they consequently killed three of our men.

The shell blasts hurled me across the ground at least twenty feet or more and dazed the living hell out of me. In fear that another barrage would come, I clung over the side of the cliff just behind me by my fingers. Luckily for me the firing ended, because the drop to the ground below was at least seventy-five feet. I seriously doubt I would have survived the fall. Our artillery's error was psychologically devastating. In addition, I had the unpleasant task of placing our dead comrades on stretchers and carrying them down the steep cliffs, which were extremely treacherous.

From our hilltop vantage point on Fonte Ridge, we could easily see all the terrain leading toward the beach. We saw several enemy soldiers engaging our men in small firefights about two hundred yards behind our lines. One unusual incident, in full view, was that four enemy soldiers, who were among the many hundreds that had broken through our lines in the attack, were hiding in a deep bomb crater. They were poised to attack a group of five or six marines that were mopping up enemy remnants but could not see them hidden just below ground level. Although we were screaming at the top of our lungs trying to warn them, they could not understand us because of the distance, and we dared not fire at the hidden enemy for fear the marines might think we were the enemy.

The hidden Japs suddenly leaped from the bomb crater and charged the marines, who were in a skirmish line with their backs turned toward the enemy. As the dumbfounded marines turned around, one of the enemy soldiers, an officer, waved his samurai sword menacingly at them. With the Japs only twenty feet or so from the marines, it looked as though they would get to them. Suddenly the marines opened fire with automatic weapons and cut four of the enemy down only a few feet short of them. In a last desperate attempt, the Jap officer tried to throw his hand grenade, but it exploded harmlessly. One of the marines ran over to pick up the officer's samurai sword and turned toward us on the ridgeline, waving it as a gesture of victory. The sword's gleaming blade glittered like a mirror in the bright morning sun.

Strong Medicine

We marines will always treasure,
From thinned out lines we gave full measure;
Strong enemy thrusts against our lines,
Were beaten back, so many times.

Those night assaults were sure no pleasure,
But now relate them at our leisure;
A thousand Japs would scream banzai,
But we held fast and they would die.

Our valuable training was well applied,
Fine marksmanship can't be denied;
To survivors of a banzai charge,
Those battle scenes were no mirage.
—The author

By late afternoon, our platoon advanced to the top of the ridge, where that morning the enemy initially started their all-out attack on us. We commenced digging new foxholes, making sure this time to dig a little deeper just in case there would be another attempt to launch one more frontal assault on our positions during the night. Thankfully, the enemy probably shot its bolt in their last attack, and the night remained uneventful.

At eight a.m., July 27, our entire front jumped off in a full-scale attack against the enemy. On this particular attack, my buddy and myself were part of a bazooka team. Moving forward approximately three hundred yards in a wide skirmish line, we unexpectedly ran smack into an enemy 77mm cannon hidden in a large hedge-type bush. The enemy lowered the barrel of their cannon in direct fire at us—some too damn close for comfort.

We spotted the enemy's weapon by the smoke it gave off after firing. We both kneeled down and prepared to take out the enemy cannon. When I loaded the bazooka's projectile, I tapped my partner on the shoulder, letting him know that the bazooka was now ready to fire. He aimed at the area where the smoke was coming from, but when he pulled the trigger, the weapon did not fire.

We crouched low in order to make a small target and noticed that the bazooka's trap door, which protected the batteries, had opened during our advance. At what point the batteries fell out, it would be impossible for us to determine. Confronted with a useless weapon, we both decided to fall back. In so doing, we stumbled onto a dugout with three officers inside who were watching our advancing units. One of the officers was none other than our commanding officer.

Our C.O. looked up at us standing there meekly. He demanded to know what we were doing back there. Stammering half coherently, we told him the sad story. Talk about catching hell! He barked out enough invectives to fill a dictionary. "Take your damn rifles and move up ahead and join F Company!" We both needed no second invitation and took off before our C.O. could finish his tirade.

Moving away quickly, we caught up with F Company. Lucky for us, we were at the tail end of the company because the marines well ahead of us were coming under heavy automatic weapons fire from the top of a long gradual sloping incline. We could easily see several marines hit by enemy fire. One marine came hobbling down the slope and dropped to the ground writhing in pain. He had been hit in the ankle. As I knelt beside him to render assistance, he asked if I had any morphine to kill the pain.

I opened the first-aid kit attached to my cartridge belt. I took out the tube of morphine, two sulfur tablets, and sulfur powder. I administered the morphine into his upper arm, and then gave him two sulfur tablets to chew on while I sprinkled the sulfur powder on his wounded ankle. As I waited a few minutes for a corpsman to arrive, I noticed how the sulfur tablets I gave him made the wounded marine's mouth and lips all chalky. I commented, "Say, pal, you're eating those tablets as though they were candy." Chiding me, the wounded marine replied, "I know that, pal, but I haven't eaten in three days." With that rejoinder, I left the marine and fortunately found my own unit, which now was advancing in a northeasterly direction, meeting no further resistance as we advanced another five hundred yards or more.

During the advance, dozens of Guam's native population streamed toward us, apparently having just escaped from captivity. One elderly gentleman approached me. I asked him in a kind of broken English, "Do you know'em where Japan man hiding positions are?" In perfect English the elderly gent succinctly replied, "No problem, marine. On our way through your lines, we passed some Japanese positions about a thousand yards back." Needless to say, I was really embarrassed. *What in the hell made me think that Guam's gentle people were not as well versed in our language as we were?* Anyway, after the elderly gentleman gave me my English lesson, the men rolled on the ground in hysterics and taunted me with remarks like "Say, you know'em where Japan men hiding?"

We stopped our advance around five p.m. and came upon a gun crew struggling to dislodge a Japanese 37mm anti-tank gun in order to place their own 37mm weapon into the same lodgment. Their weapon was currently in a position about fifty feet high that overlooked a wide area of open terrain. The ground on every side of the weapon sloped downhill, with a dirt road below circling halfway around our elevated position. But fifty feet to the left of the dug-in 37mm was a deep bowl-shaped ravine full of scrub brush and small bushes on every side of its steep slopes. I happened to notice a cave entrance that was still open on the left side of the ravine's slope just above the bottom of the ravine. I was curious enough to ask my squad sergeant why that particular cave entrance did not have its entrance blown up in order to seal it. Up to now, this was common procedure.

When the 37mm anti-tank gun was finally in place, my squad sergeant asked me on what side of the anti-tank gun I would like to dig my foxhole in order to give its gun crew added protection during the night. As I pondered his question, I kept looking down at the cave opening at the bottom of the ravine. Naturally suspicious, I told the sergeant I would dig my foxhole on the right side of the 37mm gun. This position would give me a clear unobstructed opening to the dirt road fifty feet below my position. Two other men would take the other side, about thirty feet to the left of the anti-tank gun. Their foxhole position would leave them only a few feet from the edge of the steep ravine.

After I finished my foxhole, I made sure to build up a dirt parapet at least a foot high around it in a horseshoe shape for added protection. I then lined up five or six hand grenades in a semicircle. Around nine p.m., our artillery units started sending up parachute flares. As each flare lit up the area, I cautiously raised my head slowly, barely above my foxhole, only shifting my eyes from left to right without moving my head, carefully observing the terrain in front of my position. When the flare went out, I slowly and cautiously lowered my head, careful not to make any jerky motions.

As I raised my head slowly again after the third flare lit up, an explosive device went off left of the dug-in anti-tank gun. The explosion's concussion momentarily stunned me. The two men in the foxhole to the left of the gun ran out of their foxhole screaming and jumped into the gun pit of the anti-tank gun. Their continued ear-piercing screams had me absolutely terrified. In half a panic, not knowing just what was happening, I leaped from my foxhole with my rifle, scrambled halfway down the hill that led to the road, and dropped into a prone position with my weapon facing in the direction of the anti-tank gun. As I lay there in the dark, my heart was pounding like a sledgehammer, waiting for what I felt was the inevitable.

Shortly, I heard my name called from the gun area, now about seventy to eighty feet uphill from me. Out of the blackness, I heard my squad sergeant calling, "Friedman, where the hell are you?" "Whatya want?" I asked in a choked voice. "Come on back up here, will ya? I know where they are!" *Damn it to hell anyway,* I thought to myself. *Am I the only man in this damn army?* Well, orders are orders, and I cautiously crept back uphill to where my sergeant was crouched. Inasmuch as it was totally dark, I was not able to fathom what was happening. I blurted out, "What in the hell happened anyway?" "Two of our men have been mortally wounded by Japs who crawled up the side of the ravine," he responded. "Those bastards dropped a grenade into their foxhole. Let's crawl out to their right side; I know just about where they are lying."

With our two men's terrifying screams still ringing in our ears, the sergeant asked if I had any grenades. I carefully crawled over to my foxhole and retrieved several. "Let's circle around to their right side, I heard them jabbering so I know about where they are." "How about us using some of the men in the gun pit?" I asked. "We can't! They are tending to the two wounded men!"

Cradling our rifles between our arms, we crawled in a semicircle just to the right front of where we felt the Japs were laying. After throwing one hand grenade each, we fired three or four rounds from our M1's toward their approximate position. Instantly, out of the darkness, came a piercing, agonizing cry. "Anonay! Anonay! Anonay!" From the tone of that shrill voice, we surmised that our rifle shots found their marks. But the bright flash from our rifles would give our position away, so we decided to circle around to their extreme left, in the shape of a horseshoe, and began engaging the enemy in a hand grenade duel that lasted most of the night.

The Japs did not know where we were both laying, and the grenades they tossed landed near the 37mm gun. The high dirt mound stopped their grenades from falling into our gun pit. After what seemed like an eternity, especially with rain falling on us all night, the first light of dawn finally came. In that first light, both of us stood up in a low crouch and advanced cautiously, rifles at the ready, toward their approximate position. We found all three of the enemy dead; apparently the grenades we tossed were right on target. All three Japs had large anti-tank mines strapped to their waists. The rifles alongside their bodies had fixed bayonets attached. Had they made their way through our position, they would have tried to attach those mines to some of our tanks, which were only a short distance behind us.

My sergeant asked me to bury the dead Japs. I found some telephone combat wire and tied their feet with it. I then dragged their lifeless bodies well behind our positions. I hastily dug a shallow grave with my entrenching shovel. I covered their bodies with only a few inches of soil. I grabbed each one of their rifles, with bayonets still fixed, and plunged them into the shallow soil covering them. Simultaneously with each plunge of their rifles into the shallow grave, I let out a bloodcurdling, anguished scream in a defiance that seemed to soothe my racked nerves.

I returned to the 37mm gun pit, but one of our men had died. The other, although badly wounded, was attended to by our company corpsman. I sat down on our anti-tank's metal rail with my face cupped in my hands. I had just about had it. Between the banzai assaults on our lines two nights ago and last night's ordeal, I could feel myself starting to fall apart. However, I fought it off. As luck would have it, our C.O. drove up in his jeep and turned to my squad sergeant and me, saying, "Pretty good hunting last night, huh, men?" At that point all I could do was stammer half coherently, "Yeah! Yeah! Yes, sir!"

The major, aware of my predicament, told me to take his jeep and our dead comrade down to graves registration on the beach. He added, "Stay there tonight, Friedman, and get a night's sleep!" "*Yes, sir!*" I promptly replied and quickly snapped out of my doldrums. After I left graves registration, I dug a foxhole only a few yards from a battery of 105mm artillery. I could not help but notice the change in the beach area. It now had mountains of stores and equipment all piled up on and around the beach.

That night, even with our artillery firing all night long, I slept like a log. By morning, I had to face reality. As I pondered the question as to how soon I would return to my outfit, I could see just about a mile or so offshore a beautiful white hospital ship. With mixed emotions kicking around in my mind, I wondered how I could wangle my way onto that hospital ship. The thought of going through another night like the last one, with the banzai attack still fresh in my mind, had me conjuring all sorts of crazy notions; no wonder my returning to the frontlines did not appeal to me. Just one more night like that, I'd probably be carried out to the hospital ship straight into the psycho ward. After I weighed my options, I knew what I had to do. By midmorning, I reluctantly, but faithfully, trudged all the way back to our frontline positions.

As I approached our dug-in positions, my squad sergeant greeted me warmly. I realized just what a fine marine he was—a real decent guy. At twenty-six years of age, he was emotionally mature, especially when making crisis decisions when the going got rough. Although there was some sporadic automatic weapons fire during the day just on the other side of the bowl-shaped ravine, our sector was fairly quiet.

Remembering the hellish nightmare the sergeant and I went through, I asked him late in the afternoon if I could by myself reconnoiter an area two hundred yards behind our position just to our right. It looked suspicious to me. I received permission to do so. I took my M1 and cautiously covered a wide circular area. Suddenly I came upon a large rectangular pit about twenty feet long, ten feet wide, and at least five feet deep. In it were a number of wicker baskets piled one on top of the other. They were at least two feet wide and four feet long and neatly rested in rows across the entire length of the pit.

I opened a basket just beneath me as I knelt down. It was filled with gleaming pieces of surgical instruments. Wow! I thought to myself as I continued opening the other baskets. They too were filled with surgical instruments, along with what looked like bottles of whiskey. As I closed the lid of one of the baskets, I noticed in the center of the pit a space about eighteen inches between two baskets, with a white sheet covering the space. I thought that it looked very suspicious.

I took no chances. I stood up, only a few feet away, and fired three rounds into the sheet. Instantly large red blotches appeared, and the sheet started to move. I stretched my rifle out to reach the sheet. I wrapped the sheet around the front side blade of my rifle and abruptly yanked it off. Barely moving, a Jap soldier was lying there. I reached down, and as I stepped onto one of the baskets for support, I grabbed him under the arm and leg and yanked him out of the pit in one quick swoop. Just then, several marines approached and curiously observed what took place.

I returned to our positions and told Sergeant Mondshein what I had discovered. He quickly asked, "Why in the hell didn't you grab some of the bottles of whiskey?" Unfortunately, I couldn't answer the question. As evening approached, he asked me if I wanted to stay in the 37mm gun pit tonight instead of my own foxhole. "Of course!" I quickly answered. "After last night's ordeal, I could use a little company!"

Around eleven p.m. I started the same ritual as the night before. As each parachute flare would light up our lines, we both raised our heads slowly and looked around. Only a few feet directly in front of our foxhole were four men, standing but crouched over. Each of them had their arms across each other's shoulders—like a football huddle. Obviously caught unexpectedly by the bright flare, they stood motionless. When the flares went out, I whispered to Sergeant Mondshein, "Did you see what I saw?" "You bet I did!" he whispered. "Do you think they were Japs?" I asked. "I'm not sure!" he responded. "That's why I didn't open fire." When another flare lit up the area, they were gone. So for both of us, it has remained an enigma. This incident probably comes under the wartime term "the fog of war."

The next day, with the sergeant's permission, I returned to the area where I found all the large wicker baskets. As I approached the area, I could see several marine personnel standing there. "Hey, you guys, I am the one who discovered all this stuff, you know!" The marines said they were from headquarters. They told me that I had found a veritable bonanza of surgical instruments and quinine. They said that this stuff would be shipped out all over the Pacific, where it would be used for those who acquired malaria. Not only that, but our own surgical instruments were practically destroyed by enemy artillery fire, and this find was absolutely unbelievable, they told me. "Well, how about a bottle or two of that whiskey?" I asked. "No way in hell, pal! This stuff is for medicinal use only!"

The next morning, on July 29, all units of the Twenty-First Regiment advanced about two or three miles in a northeasterly direction toward the Tumon Bay area. We reached the capital town of Agana. Our company advanced in two columns on each side of the main road leading out of the town. The devastation was awesome, with all of the town's main buildings in shambles, caused mostly by our own naval gunfire and aerial bombardments. The road leading out of the capital town was heavily mined, and some casualties were incurred by some of our leading elements. Others of our advanced patrols were well ahead of our own unit in order to test enemy strength. The annihilation of enemy forces, in their previous suicide attacks and our own counterattacks beyond Fonte Hill, seemed to be the turning point for our units in the total rout of the disorganized Japanese forces.

The dirt roads leading out of Agana were extremely dry and dusty because of the lack of rain but became very muddy when it rained. Our own column advanced about three miles out of Agana and finally halted at a crossroads. Major Houser decided around six p.m. to have us dig in temporarily for the night in a grassy field some fifty to seventy-five feet from the crossroads. While we were sitting on our steel helmets, opening our "scrumptious" K-rations, without warning an enemy tank suddenly rumbled down the road and stopped just short of the crossroads. It turned its turret toward us and opened fire with two or three rounds from its 47mm cannon. The shells exploded all around us as we scrambled for the nearest hole. Immediately after, the damn tank just turned around and scooted back up the dirt road out of sight, unscathed.

Luckily no one was hit, but the major was pissed to the gills. He slammed his steel helmet to the ground. He looked around and, as usual, spotted Sergeant Mondshein and me. "Mondshein!" the major yelled, "You and Friedman hook up the 37 anti-tank gun and take it up that road a way and dig it in just off the road. If that damn tank returns, blast it!" "Yes, sir!" we both answered in unison. Without finishing our K-rations, the sergeant and I hooked up the anti-tank gun to a jeep and towed it up the road about two hundred yards. We manhandled the weapon into the scrubby field, at least fifty yards in from the road, working feverishly to dig the weapon in before it became dark.

We cut away many low twigs and small branches that blocked our view from the road. Finally the gun was dug into a pit about three feet deep and at least eight or nine feet square. All the while, as we were digging in the weapon, a sneaky Jap sniper kept popping away at us every so often. His shots harmlessly struck the dirt parapet with which we had encircled our weapon for added protection. We made sure to keep low to avoid the sniper's fire. About nine p.m., a violent thunderstorm added to our misery with frequent flashes of lightning and high winds all around us.

Thoroughly drenched despite my poncho, while sitting on the weapon's metal gun rails, I suddenly felt a sharp stinging pain in my buttocks. I leaped up from the metal rail and yelled at the top of my lungs, "Mondshein! Mondshein! I'm hit!" "Where?" he asked. "In the ass!" I cried out. He told me to lower my trousers so he could check me out with his cigarette lighter, so I laid down in the two to three inches of water that had already entered our gun pit. "I can't find any wound," he said. "Well, what in the hell was that sharp sting I felt?" "You dumb ass, what you felt was an electric charge going through the gun from that lightning bolt!"

Wow, was I relieved! I apologized for my panicky outburst. As an afterthought, I said, "You know, sarge, lucky for us the major did not come up here to inspect our site just at the moment you were looking down with my fully exposed white ass. Who knows what in the hell he would have thought!" In either case, that minor operation to get the Jap tank was an exercise in futility because the enemy tank never returned.

We pushed north toward Tumon Bay, and all units were making large sweeps through terrain much different than the Fonte Plateau sector. At this time large areas had considerable denser growth. With patrol actions now on a larger scale than before into heavy jungle terrain, and with very light opposition in the last phases of the campaign, our units advanced to the most northern sector of Guam and reached Ritidian Point, with its towering cliffs up to six hundred feet high overlooking the sea. Finally, on August 10, all organized resistance by the enemy had ended.

Guam's gallant native population can now look back with justifiable pride and honor in the valor of the resistance they so nobly exhibited during the entire two and a half years of a bitter Japanese occupation as well as the loyal support they gave our forces during the entire campaign. There is no doubt that a solid bond between us marines and Guam's people, forged during the struggle to return the island to its people, was and will always be unshakable.

With the campaign officially over, we took on the task of setting up our new campsite in an area of northern Guam only a short distance from where our Seabee battalions had started construction of an enormous airfield for the B-29s that were expected sometime around November. When our new campsite was in place, we received new replacements for the anticipated patrols we would be making soon in order to flush out a few thousand of the enemy's forces who had retreated into jungle hideouts mostly in Guam's northern sector.

From our new campsite, our patrol actions would be in full platoon strength, lasting from four to six hours. These combat patrols would take place by September, and if necessary, we would take vehicles to points most advantageous in order to fulfill each mission to the fullest extent. Our orders were to destroy any remnants of the enemy that our patrols would come in contact with.

Of the fifty or so combat patrols our company engaged in between late August 1944 and the first week of November, many had unique memorable incidents. Fortunately for our new replacements, they learned from our firsthand experience what they did not get during the first phase of the campaign. Being with combat experienced men, it was easier for these new replacements to adjust to the rigors of daily actions they would be seeing—much like on-the-job training.

In one of my first patrol actions with our third platoon, I was given the point position. The point man on a patrol normally is out front of the platoon some ten to twenty yards in order to forewarn the patrol of any possible imminent contact with an enemy. Usually just arm and hand signals sufficed. On this patrol, however, I fell back to tell my lieutenant that I could see up ahead something moving in one of the native huts. Spread out in a skirmish line, we steadily advanced forward through a large coconut grove area toward the native hut.

I was the first to reach the shabby hut, which was built up on wooden stilts with a thatched roof and wooden floor that was at least six feet off the ground. The moving object I saw was an enemy soldier. Just as I approached, he stood up, walked to the edge, put a rope around his neck, and jumped off in an attempt to hang himself. I quickly took my Kabar knife from its sheath, and reaching up, cut the rope from his neck. He then fell about six feet to the ground.

As the rest of my platoon came up, the Jap started screaming in Japanese with his arms raised; it seemed to me as though he was pleading not to be killed. Because of his persistent screaming, my lieutenant ordered me to shoot him. I noticed on the chest of the enemy soldier a large swath of cotton that was obviously covering a large chest wound. The Jap continued to yell at the top of his voice, so the lieutenant ordered me a second time: "Damn it, Friedman, kill him! He's calling out to his buddies!" "I don't think so, sir," I replied. "The little guy is pleading for his life. Why don't we take him back for interrogation?" I asked. But the lieutenant was adamant. For a third time he ordered me in no uncertain terms to kill him. One of the Japanese words I had learned was the order to "keep quiet." When I yelled at him in Japanese to shut up, he did so promptly.

Not wanting it on my conscience to kill a wounded man, I repeated over again for us to take the prisoner back to camp for interrogation. This time our platoon leader relented. On the long slow march back to our camp area, our platoon stopped along a dusty road for rations. The prisoner was now sitting alongside of me, and he started quietly to adjust his untidy cloth leggings, making sure not to make any eye contact with any of us.

As I opened my K-ration tin containing American cheese, I offered him a portion of it. Before accepting the cheese, he turned to us with his hands clasped together and motioned to all of us as a measure of thanks. He took the cheese from me and proceeded to eat it in a most dainty manner. When I offered him some water from my canteen, one of the men blurted out, "You're not going to let him drink from your canteen, are you, Friedman?" I poured some water into a half-section of a tin that the cheese came in. The prisoner went through the same ritual with his hands clasped toward us as an expression of thanks.

The trek back to camp took us about an hour. When the lieutenant and I reached Major Houser's tent, the major demanded to know from the lieutenant why the patrol returned so soon. When the major finished reading the "riot act" to our platoon leader, he turned to me and said, "Okay, Friedman, bring your boy along; we'll take him down to regimental headquarters for interrogation." A five-minute ride on a muddy road to regimental headquarters led us to a tent where a marine officer interpreter questioned the prisoner, who was more relaxed when faced by someone who spoke his language.

With each question the marine interpreter asked, the prisoner would point to me. After two or three times of his finger pointing, I cut in and asked the interpreter why in the hell the Jap kept pointing toward me "He is only answering my questions as to how he was captured; that's why he keeps pointing toward you." After the questioning was over, they gave the prisoner some coffee and a doughnut. Again he went through the same ritual with his clasped hands in appreciation. When asked when he had eaten last, the prisoner said he had not eaten in five days.

I learned from my squad sergeant months later why I didn't make a corporal rating like the other men. Sergeant Mondshein quietly explained to me that because our platoon returned from the patrol early, and because of the reprimand our lieutenant received for it, the lieutenant had pledged that I would never make another rate. The lieutenant sure kept his word. The odd thing about this entire incident was that our lieutenant never once showed the slightest animosity toward me. I can now look back with satisfaction and a clear conscience in that I did not kill an unarmed wounded prisoner.

On Patrol

The Lieutenant and I disagree,
About the enemy captured by me;
Should we end this patrol and turn in our prize,
I assumed his answer was just disguise;
And not amusing to me, as you will see.

You returned the patrol early, our C.O. would roar,
We both could say nothing,
Just stared meekly in awe.
He chewed out the louie, his language was blunt,
I felt my lieutenant won't forgive this affront;
But he masked his indifference, so cleverly from me,
My lieutenant made sure I'd remain PFC.
—The author

In 1994, I returned to Guam for the fiftieth anniversary of Guam's liberation. It was called "The Golden Salute!" The wonderful people of Guam honored us with a series of parades and events in our honor. I, however, sought some clarification on a very controversial subject concerning a former navy radioman first class named George Tweed. He was the only American survivor when the Japanese captured Guam. Mr. Tweed, with the help of the island's citizenry, managed to elude capture from the enemy for thirty-one months.

The enemy knew Mr. Tweed was on the island and were intent on capturing him. With many harrowing incidents, Guam's Chamorros risked their own lives to shelter and feed him, managing cleverly to prevent his capture. Mr. Tweed ultimately saved himself by signaling one of our destroyers on July 10, 1944, and was picked up by a shore party from the destroyer in the nick of time.

At the hotel where I was staying when I returned to Guam for the celebration, I met an elderly employee on the hotel's staff. I asked him if he would provide me with some answers to a series of questions concerning radioman Tweed. There are two perspectives about the Tweed saga that need to be aired. On the one side, the gentleman I interviewed told me that Mr. Tweed represented the United States as a living symbol and that is why the civilian population helped by secretly hiding him, even though the risk was great. With a price on his head, anyone the Japanese caught hiding Mr. Tweed would face immediate execution.

On the other hand, the gentleman told me that radioman Tweed allowed the Chamorros to suffer murder and torture while he continued to remain protected and supported by the Chamorros in Guam's secret jungle hideouts. As U.S. forces approached invasion, the enemy increased their efforts to capture Tweed. Consequently, they beheaded several civilians for not providing the whereabouts of Tweed's hiding places. The controversy still exists as to whether saving the life of Mr. Tweed as a symbol was worth the lives of so many civilians who suffered for protecting him.

Interestingly, Mr. Tweed was instrumental in leading one of our own platoons on a patrol. He was very knowledgeable about the island's hideouts and caves, used by the enemy to evade capture by our forces.

It wasn't very often that our patrols turned out to be humorous, but on this one, an unusual incident was quite memorable. As our platoon was making its way through heavy undergrowth, the lead man brushed by some overhanging branches of a large bush. Out came a swarm of wasps that dove on all of us from all directions. What a sight we must have been, with all the ooches and ouches from the entire platoon slapping away and jumping up and down in a frantic jig that probably looked like an Indian war dance to any onlooker. Fortunately, the enemy wasn't around, because we would have been cold meat under the circumstances.

After those heavy downpours, the dirt roads would hold large puddles of water for days. My foxhole was just off a dirt road from which I had a view of over a hundred yards just in case some enemy stragglers unexpectedly came into view. With the road covered with dozens of water-filled puddles, I heard an unusual sound of a plop, plop, plop, which continued to come closer with each plop. Taking no chances, I leveled my rifle in anticipation of some possible enemy action, but discovered much to my chagrin all this plopping was being made by very large bullfrogs, which always showed up after the heavy rains.

As the evening wore on, I could feel something irritating me under the tongue of my field shoe. As it was now dark, all I could do was feel the area with my finger. The affected area had a tick, which obviously was feeding away on my blood for who knows how long. Anyway, not able to use any light, I just yanked it off, but the damn thing left a portion of its head just under the skin and the area, which kept me scratching for months.

Many of our patrols made in the Pati Point sector were very difficult, and contact with the enemy was frequent. It seems that the enemy chose this particular area because of its many caves and thick jungle, affording them with excellent cover. The enemy also took refuge beneath the cliff's ridgeline, making it very difficult to root them out.

As our third platoon approached the cliffs, we could hear a chopping sound coming only a short distance ahead of us. Our platoon leader ordered a few men, who happened to be leading our platoon, to advance and see just what the hacking noise was all about, while the rest of us just kneeled down along the jungle trail and waited. In less than thirty seconds, several bursts of automatic weapons fire broke the silence, and with that, one of the enemy ran right by me—running at top speed to boot.

I jumped up and took chase after the fleeing Jap. I was able to follow him because he was leaving blood on all the jungle plant leaves. I must have chased him for at least a hundred yards and finally found him lying motionless in a small clearing. I called to the rest of the men that I had found him and, assuming that the Jap was dead, they took a smoking break. Not being a smoker, I kept glancing at the enemy's prostrate body and thought I noticed some small movement.

I turned to Sergeant Mondshein and said, "I think the Jap is still alive!" All he said was "Well, finish him off, Friedman!" "Hey, sarge! I haven't fired my weapon, and for one shot, I'll have to clean the weapon back at camp." With that the Sarge fired a single shot, and when the body was turned over, the Jap had his hand in the upper pocket of his shirt on a grenade. Luckily for us all, I wasn't a smoker and had the good sense to be extra cautious.

With our new campsite set up nicely, the men spent each Sunday either attending church services, taking care of personal things like washing clothes, or just relaxing. I, for one, enjoyed relaxing at the beach. Just offshore, no more than thirty feet or so, were large chunks of coral in no more than three feet of water. I turned the coral over. Clinging to the coral were small seashells with a light green surface, surrounded by an orange ring. Clusters of those very pretty seashells, called cat's-eyes, would cling to the bottom of the coral and were very easy to pull off. I put them, by the hundreds, in my steel helmet.

Often as I waded through the seaweed, sea snakes would dart out and quickly swim away. Although they were supposed to be very poisonous, they never were aggressive and I just ignored them. On one large piece of coral that had a deep crevice, a baby octopus was hiding. I gently grabbed it and put it in my steel helmet, which I filled with water. It was amazing how this little creature would dart back and forth in every direction; the iridescent colors as the sun shone on it were positively brilliant. Another large chunk of coral in a similar crevice held a small three-inch fish that was dark pink in color. Not being very familiar with these fish specimens, I decided not to pick it up. Some years later, while leafing through a large dictionary, I noticed a picture of the identical fish, and the notation said they were extremely poisonous.

Back at camp, I dumped hundreds of the cat's-eyes under a coconut tree, where large red ants would eat the flesh. Then, in order to give the shells some luster, I soaked them in shaving lotion alcohol. Guam's Chammoro women were excellent craftswomen, and for twenty dollars, they would sew the shells on the sides of lovely pink pocketbooks they made. Our men would send these lovely pocketbooks home to their families. Some of the mail from home not only mentioned how delighted they were to receive them, but also how expensive similar seashell pocketbooks were at the better department stores.

One day several native children, with their mothers, approached our campsite and asked our officers if they could sing some island homespun songs to honor the men.

The officer replied that his men would feel honored to listen to the children give a rendition of their island's homespun songs. To say the least, our tough, battle-hardened men were very touched by their offer. It was this one version though that the men found quite apropos.

> *On a Monday morning, the action came to Guam,*
> *Eighth of December, nineteen forty-one;*
> *Mr. Sam, Sam, my dear ole Uncle Sam,*
> *Won't you please come back to Guam.*

> *We don't like their sake,*
> *We like C-A-N-A-D-I-A-N,*
> *We don't want the Japanese,*
> *It's better A-M-E-R-I-C-A-N;*
> *Mr. Sam, Sam, our dear ole Uncle Sam,*
> *We want you please come back to Guam.*

One of our men in the company, a consummate loner who rarely spoke to anyone, had one of the strangest quirks imaginable. Each night, shortly after taps, he would secretly leave camp and penetrate deep into the jungle to hunt down enemy stragglers and shoot them in their hideouts.

With killer instincts that were so frightening, not even our officers made any attempt to stop him on his nightly forays. On the night I had the ten p.m. to two a.m. guard watch around our camp's perimeter, I saw him leave his tent with his rifle and hand grenades attached to his cartridge belt.

With my curiosity aroused, I decided to follow him. I entered the jungle at the point where he had entered, and I carefully followed the narrow footpath, which was probably made by his nightly trips. After some hundred yards or so, without the slightest warning, he bolted out from behind a large tree just off the trail and forcefully thrust his rifle across my chest, pinning me. In a menacing voice he snarled, "Where in the hell do you think you're going?" I was so startled I could barely speak. "N-n-n-no-where!" I meekly croaked. "Well, old buddy, you just get your ass back to camp, and I mean now!"

When he released his rifle from my chest, I took off without a word, making it back to camp about midnight in record time. I returned to my guard duty, and I said nothing to anyone about the incident. Incidentally he was ultimately killed on Iwo Jima while singlehandedly rushing a machine gun nest.

Guam Poker

One may possibly ask, "What is the chance of receiving some bodily injuries from a poker game?" If the question sounds a bit ludicrous, so be it. It could have occurred. Nevertheless, this one poker game incident pales by comparison to our daily patrol actions.

I am referring to our ubiquitous poker and blackjack games, played nightly in our company tents on our sleeping cots. When our lights went out at ten p.m. after taps sounded, the card games continued by placing a few candles at each end of our cots. Many card games continued until dawn.

In the five card draw poker game I played with four other marines, the money pots at times were sizable. This incident started off innocently enough. The dealer, who sat next to me, dealt me a perfect ace to five straight flush in spades. "Man, what luck!" the men blurted out.

When the deal passed to me, I made sure to shuffle the deck and had the cards cut. Innocently, as I started to deal, I remarked, "Well, fellas, as long as I am dealing, I may as well give myself another straight flush."

As God is my witness, that is precisely what happened. I actually dealt myself an identical straight flush. When I looked at my cards, I was absolutely shocked. For the moment I was tempted to throw the hand in for fear of repercussions by the other players, but I played the hand anyway.

I decided not to raise the pot and take advantage of this unbelievable stroke of luck. Still, when my cards were disclosed, I was vehemently accused of being a card shark. I kept swearing up and down that this was nothing more than a fantastic coincidence. The men relented somewhat, but they still grumbled well after the incident.

With our daily combat patrols still going on, every man had slung his fully loaded rifle under his sleeping cot, a conscious thought that did not escape me at that time.

Unfortunately, another strange and perplexing incident happened on patrol; I felt compelled once more to disobey a direct order from my lieutenant. While our platoon patrolled about a hundred yards from the beach, the marine just ahead of me spotted a single Jap running along a fifteen-foot high ridge and, with one burst from his B.A.R., cut him down. Three of us ran up the steep incline in pursuit and spotted the Jap crouched in a small recess in the hillside. The poor guy had a portion of his mouth and lips shot away. As he looked up at us, he pointed to one of the hand grenades attached to my cartridge belt. I thought he wanted the grenade so he could take his life.

With the rest of our platoon some thirty feet below us, our lieutenant asked, "What's going on up there, Friedman?" "We have a wounded Jap, sir!" I responded. "Well, Friedman, kill him; we have to move out now!" Not wanting the killing of a wounded man on my conscience, I once again said, "Let's bring him back for interrogation, sir." "I gave you a direct order; kill him, now!" As I continued to stall, the marine next to me put the enemy soldier out of his misery.

When I climbed down from the ridge, the lieutenant started chewing me out and angrily said he would put me on report for disobeying a direct order. Whether or not the lieutenant turned me in, I never knew; that was the last I ever heard of the incident. To this very day, I never regretted my decision. It only proved to me that under highly unusual circumstances in combat, as a matter of conscience, even a direct order from a superior may be rejected.

By mid-October, the bomber airstrip under construction not far from our camp became an attraction for us. On our Sundays off, some of us would take a jeep and drive down and watch the Seabees and Army Engineers put the finishing touches on the lengthy runway. It must have been close to ten thousand feet long in order to accommodate the heavily laden bombers' ability to take off safely. A few weeks later, some of the sleekest looking planes flew in and landed with a great amount of fanfare. Those shiny B-29s were absolutely awesome in appearance; and by comparison, the other bombers looked puny. When the wind direction was right, the B-29s would fly directly over our campsite not much more than a thousand feet before gaining altitude. Knowing they had a full bomb load made it a little more than frightening as they roared overhead on their way to Japan.

Guam's civilian population was tragically dislocated after marine and army forces practically leveled all of the island's buildings while trying to destroy the enemy forces. Private houses were in shambles caused by our pre-invasion aerial and artillery bombardment.

People were living either in tents or hastily constructed huts made from any lumber or corrugated metal that could be found. Those temporary living quarters dotted the island's landscape until new housing for the civilian population was constructed.

Our new campsite, from where we made our daily combat patrols, was only a few hundred yards from a small hut that housed a family that included three teenage daughters and their mother. Every other day, one of the girls came into our camp in order to have an ulcer on her leg treated by our medical corpsman.

Because of a heavy downpour, the dirt road leaving from our campsite was pocked with pools of water and mud. I was asked by the corpsman to drive the teenager to her house because the footing on the muddy road was too dangerous.

Our jeep had no trouble negotiating the muddy road, and in two minutes we arrived at her family's hut. Her mother, standing in the open doorway, thanked me and asked if I would care to come inside for a cool drink. Not wishing to hurt her feelings, I thanked her and told her that I could stay only a few minutes.

A very friendly conversation ensued, and I was amazed with the full command of English that this lovely lady had. I quickly mentioned that I had already overstayed my visit. She then asked me if I would like to return for dinner that evening. I was a little reluctant, but agreed even though I knew the native quarters were temporarily restricted.

I waited until it was dark enough and cautiously made my way so as not to be seen. I was warmly greeted by the family and was seated at a small wooden table. I watched the girls holding the skewered pieces of meat over an open wooden fire. I could not help but notice how angelic the girls' faces appeared in the glow of the fire.

An after-dinner conversation ensued with the family. One of the mother's questions was what my religious persuasion was. I mentioned that I was of the Jewish faith and noticed a somewhat perplexed look on the woman's face. She then made a comment that I was unable to comprehend the meaning of. Consequently I was unable to give an appropriate response.

An hour with this lovely family just flew by, and I thanked everyone for their gracious hospitality. As I was leaving, this kind and gentle woman asked me if I would like to return for a visit when I had a chance. I replied that I would if I could.

Without a valid reason, I decided not to revisit this gracious family. A few weeks later, one of our men handed me a letter written by the family I had visited. In beautiful handwriting, the letter asked why I had not attempted to communicate or revisit and asked if she had in any way hurt my feelings during my visit. The letter closed by saying that "to err is human, but to forgive is divine!"

I have spent a lifetime regretting my immature behavior and hope and pray that an admission of my youthful indiscretion will serve as a catharsis to help alleviate the stigma I have lived with so many years.

Returning from patrol one day, I noticed my foot had developed a bad blister from the sand in my wet field shoes. I took cover in my pup tent, where I made a quick inspection of my foot. The damn blister was the size of a half-dollar and throbbed painfully. In order to get some relief, I had to keep my field shoe off. As I hobbled along toward the chow line, a voice behind me asked, "What's wrong with your foot, Friedman?" With my foot throbbing, I couldn't hear and did not respond to the question. Once more and with more authority, "What's wrong with your foot, Friedman?"

Turning halfway around, I saw that it was Major Houser. Caught totally unaware, I stammered, "M-m-m, m-y-y f-f-foot, s-s-sir! It has a bad painful blister," I responded. I thought I detected a faint smile under his large mustache at my apparent nervousness. He quickly checked my sore ankle and told me to see the corpsman and get it treated. Since I was not able to wear my field shoe on the blistered foot, the corpsman gave me light duty for the next few days. I just hung around our small bivouac encampment doing mess duty, which was a heck of a lot safer than going on patrol.

Later on, when our third platoon returned from patrol, my lieutenant ordered me, as a precautionary measure, to walk the perimeter of our encampment while the men were having chow. I disappeared into the heavy jungle undergrowth about fifty yards or so with my M1 and slowly circled the encampment in the eerie stillness. I could still hear the men jabbering away on the chow line. With my ankle still throbbing, I decided to take a break. I leaned against a tree and admittedly started daydreaming somewhat. Without any warning, a Jap brandishing a menacingly held bayonet charged out of the jungle directly toward me.

Christ, was I startled! I quickly backed away from him in order to put some distance between us. I lowered my rifle, and from the hip I fired the entire clip as he charged toward me. He dropped right in front of my feet. When I looked down at him, his eyes were wide open and looking toward the sky. But he was dead. Standing over his prostrate body, I must have muttered over and over again, "You Jap bastard!" In no more than thirty seconds, a few of our men ran over to see what happened. I could barely give a coherent account of what precisely took place. I hobbled back to my pup tent, but the lingering effect of the incident and the stress it created traumatized me for the entire night.

Returning to our main camp the next day, we all were happy to leave the Pati Point area. We returned to a little more normalcy and had a chance to shower, clean our fatigues, and eat better food. Just my luck I caught guard duty the very first night back.

While we stopped for a short break close to a heavily wooded area, after partaking in our "tasty" k-rations, I hesitate to mention it but I had a sudden urge to relieve myself. I removed my entrenching shovel from my upper pack and disappeared into the dense jungle. I was certain to take my M1 along, just in case, because no soldier will deny how vulnerable we are in a squatting position.

I soon became aware of a heavy buzzing sound a short distance away. About a hundred feet away, I came upon a dead Japanese officer. His shoulder insignia indicated that he at least held the rank of major. The thousands of blowflies that hovered over the corpse acted as a deterrent and prevented me from even attempting to turn his body over in order to retrieve his samurai sword and pistol.

I returned to our temporary encampment, and I didn't say anything about what I had seen, thinking that I would return to the sight later. Some ten minutes later, one of our men excitedly appeared from the jungle brandishing the samurai sword and pistol. After he drew the sword from its scabbard and flaunted it, we were amazed at its quality and beauty. Today's market for such a prize would bring me a nice price. In retrospect, I still reminisce about what might have been.

We all took a more serious approach this time, even though our area was relatively safe. There was a rash of break-ins by enemy stragglers. The commissary storerooms were being broken into during the night, and it was mostly our canned food that was being stolen by a half-starved enemy.

One night on guard duty, at approximately three a.m., I was alerted to an unusual sound emanating from the area of our commissary storeroom. The fifteen-by-fifteen-foot storeroom presented no problem for anyone attempting to break in, being surrounded only by screened wiring. As I approached stealthily, in total darkness, with my rifle at the ready, two or three forms bolted from the enclosure like scared rabbits. I fired my M1 at the fleeing forms but with no apparent hits.

Those shots must have awakened half the camp. In seconds, the sergeant of the guard arrived and asked me what in the hell happened. We looked around the commissary to see if anything had been taken. Nothing seemed to be missing except the perpetrators. By morning, though, the men in my platoon subjected me to a rash of spirited ribbing, with remarks such as "Friedman shoots at phantom enemy!" And "Trigger-happy Friedman does it again!" All I could do was to take it in stride.

In a more serious vein, though, our second platoon came back early one afternoon after running into an ambush. One of our men was killed, but they were unable to retrieve his body.

The C.O. ordered our third platoon, along with some of our men in the second platoon, to guide us to the firefight area. Fortunately we were able to ultimately retrieve our dead comrade, and the second platoon men carried him back. It wasn't a routine operation, though.

We advanced very cautiously into the area where the ambush took place. We came under fire from the enemy hidden between the roots of a banyan tree. The wall of the tree's roots offered the Japs excellent cover. Lying side by side with our men in the prone position, our firing was ineffective. We were still not aware that the Japs had captured the M1 rifle from the dead marine. Suddenly, a volley of four or five shots in quick succession, inches above my head, clipped the twigs of the small bush I was lying under.

Our lieutenant, a recent arrival from the states and obviously frustrated, broke the silence and hollered out, "Let's charge 'em!" The marine on my left, with a B.A.R., was unable to fire his weapon on automatic. He shouted back at the green lieutenant, "You out of your friggen mind, sir?" With the marine only able to fire his automatic weapon in single shots, I angrily grabbed the B.A.R. from him saying, "Give me that damn thing!" I attempted to make a quick adjustment on the weapon. I stood up in a low crouch and pulled the trigger, but the weapon would not fire on automatic. I tossed the B.A.R. back at the unsuspecting marine lying there and blurted out, "Here, take this piece of crap, will ya!"

Minutes later, there were two explosions in the area of the banyan tree, and shattered debris fell on some of the men around us. Moving forward cautiously, we found two dead Japs. They had committed suicide with their own hand grenades. While going through their personal items, I found three chicken eggs and very carefully placed them in my fatigues pocket without saying a word to anyone. Upon our return to camp, I wasted no time disappearing into the jungle with my mess gear and fried them. Being very hungry, I was careful not to give myself away. Fresh eggs were worth their weight in diamonds, and I wasn't about to share those eggs with anyone. As I stepped back out from the heavy undergrowth, one of our men asked, "Hey, Friedman, where in the hell were you anyway?" "Oh, I just stepped into the bushes to take a leak." "Yeah?" he answered. "Be more careful next time. For a moment I thought you were a Jap!"

On Patrol

Stay alert men, the platoon leader said,
Enemy positions are just up ahead;
Our nerves are taut, and stomachs queasy,
Many times before this, it never gets easy
All eyes strained in the dim jungle lightness,
Those camouflaged Japs are practically sightless;
Grim looks on our faces, better beware,
Caught in ambush from the enemy's lair.
—The author

An afterthought occurred to me while I was frying the eggs. I wondered just how those Japs got those eggs. Being an old farmhand, I surmised the native huts that had been abandoned had hens roosting there. Making a short reconnaissance from our camp, I found an old abandoned hut. Inside, high on one of the wooden rafters, a hen was cackling away. I climbed at least fifteen feet or more to reach the nest and shooed the hen away and retrieved three eggs. I made the mistake of telling some of our guys my good fortune, and had to share those hard-earned eggs this time or become "persona non grata" or possibly worse.

Once again we left by trucks for the Pati Point area, with its high cliffs that were honeycombed with enemy dugouts. As we approached the steep cliff area, we suddenly came under fire from a well-entrenched enemy and engaged them in a fierce firefight.

Our determined automatic weapons fire and our grenade attacks into their hidden dugouts finally drove eight of the enemy out. At that point we were able to cut them down.

Inspecting the inside of the deep dugout, we discovered four women—three Japanese and one fairly young Chamorran woman. It was she who told us that she was kept prisoner. All four were very unkempt and ill-fed. On the way back to our campsite, the pretty Chamorran woman told me that her name was Jong. She was a nurse before the war and worked for our navy as a nurse. The three Japanese women seemed to be in their twenties. When we returned to camp, the men were agog with curiosity and made snide comments like, "Hey! Did you guys make out with the Jap women?" Of course, we lied just to tease them.

Several weeks later, I heard that Jong was working at the naval hospital in Agana. I kept this bit of information from the others. One Sunday I left camp and hitched a ride into Agana, hoping to locate her at the navy hospital. I asked the attendant to have Jong paged. When she arrived, I was surprised to see how pretty she looked in her clean white uniform.

Jong greeted me warmly, and I was surprised that she remembered me. She spoke to me of her long ordeal in captivity, and how the fact that she was a nurse helped in keeping her alive. When I asked if she would go to the movies with me, she said apologetically that she already had a date that evening with a navy doctor. I realized that I was out of my league. I bid her good luck and a fond farewell. When I returned to camp, I said absolutely nothing to anyone. Not wanting to become bombarded with dozens of inquisitive questions and possible taunting, I decided to keep it my own secret.

By the middle of October, headquarters made a decision in an attempt to get the remaining enemy stragglers, who were still hiding out in the cave entrances on the towering cliffsides overlooking Ritidian Point. Our third platoon boarded three alligator landing craft, fully armed, and traveled along the coastline several miles. Other marine personnel traveled with us, carrying sound amplifier equipment.

Our platoon was there to protect them as they set up their amplifiers, which faced the high cliffs just in from the beach. A marine officer oversaw as one or two Japanese prisoners implored their well-hidden comrades over the loudspeaker to give themselves up. They were promised that they would be given good treatment, food, and medical care. Unbelievably, about a dozen or more of the enemy made their way down from the rugged sheer cliffs and surrendered. It sure was a pitiful sight to see those half-starved, emaciated remnants of the enemy.

Combat Patrols

Guam, August–November 1944

On Pacific island jungle trails,
Trees still whisper many tales;
Of daring men in jungle greens,
With silent stealth, they were marines.

Few words were spoken by the men,
Hand signals only, more than ten;
And knowing not what lay in store,
Though well prepared for total war.

From out their caves, with hands held high,
Not all the enemy wished to die;
Combat patrols were surely active,
The rarest sight though, was to see a captive.
—The author

Hooray! It was official! ... "As of November 3, 1944, all combat patrols will be terminated." The remaining enemy remnants were left to wither on the proverbial vine. Since the Guam campaign ended in mid-August, patrol actions to extirpate enemy holdouts cost our company approximately twenty-five casualties, either killed or wounded. Our company alone had killed well over three hundred enemy holdouts.

With dozens of new replacements arriving, a new training program was being implemented. Interestingly, I am certain that our national newspapers back home gave wide notice in their headlines when Guam fell to our forces back in August. But they probably revealed little about our daily hazardous patrol actions during the following weeks.

From our new campsite, one of the duties given to the men on a rotation basis was garbage patrol. One man, with his rifle, accompanied the garbage truck each day on its trip to our local garbage dumpsite. On the one and only trip I made, the dirt road leading into the dumpsite was pocked with deep water-filled holes, which made it necessary to prop oneself up against the truck's cab to prevent falling off the truck as it heaved from side to side.

As our vehicle approached a large garbage mound, three enemy stragglers leaped from the garbage heap and scooted lickety-split into the dense jungle. I leveled my rifle from the roof of the cab. However, it was impossible to steady my weapon while the truck bounced up and down. It bounced so violently that all four rounds I fired at the fleeing Japs went astray.

Without hesitation, like a hound dog chasing after a rabbit, I leaped from the truck and gave chase after the fleeing quarry into the dense undergrowth. With extreme caution, I stealthily combed the area, all the while thinking to myself, *just what in the hell am I doing here all alone?*

Detecting a faint smell of smoke, I followed my nose in the direction of a small clearing, where I discovered a small rickety wooden table with warm food on it. No doubt, the Japs scrounged the food from the garbage heap. I took no chances. Now that I was in the open, I took the butt of my rifle and smashed the wooden table, scattering the food to the ground, and got out of there. I quickly made my way back to the truck, which was still parked by the garbage mound.

I was greeted coolly by the driver, who unloaded on me a heavy dose of sarcasm. "You know, Friedman, I had to unload this damn filthy garbage all alone. Besides which, I'll be damned if I would have chased after those Japs by myself." "Sorry if I upset you," I responded, but my apology fell on deaf ears and failed to soothe his ruffled feathers. Consequently I was met with a stony silence from the driver all the way back to camp. I thought it best not to broach the incident any further.

By mid-November, all those rumors about going home became a reality, but they were only partially true. For those of us who made it through the Bougainville and Guam campaigns, a select few would be going back stateside; those chosen to go home were the men who were married and those who had children. Needless to say, we single guys felt betrayed, and it was a crushing disappointment. Of course, the reason given was that we experienced men had to stay on as a cadre that would help train the new inexperienced replacements.

The new training program was a farce to us old-timers. Here we were, crawling under barbed wire with live ammo being fired over our heads. For us, having to engage in those exercises was nothing short of stupidity. Having gone through all those months of action, who in the hell needed this?

As the weeks and months passed, Guam changed dramatically, hardly recognizable by comparison with only a short time before.

Admiral Nimitz had moved his headquarters from Hawaii to Guam, and the military buildup of Guam's port and dock facilities with mountains of arms and heavy building equipment was staggering.

As the weeks of intensified training ensued, we were also given a wider latitude of time off for the more mundane aspects in our daily routines, including those ubiquitous, omnipresent poker and blackjack card games. However, the ever-present realization of a third campaign was very disquieting, especially now that at least 20 percent of our experienced men had gone home. Their experience in any upcoming campaign would be sorely missed.

By mid-December 1944, our company was shown aerial photographs of Iwo Jima. By January 1945, we knew that island would be our next campaign. Preliminary information of Iwo's defenses showed that the island was well-fortified, but our officers told us that the seventy-two days of air and sea bombardment would neutralize the island's defenses and we would face only a three-day campaign. Those aerial photographs could not possibly show how the island was honeycombed with deep underground caves and defenses so deep that all the preliminary bombardment barely scratched them.

On the morning of February 15, 1945, our company broke camp. With elements of our third battalion, we made the forced march of twelve miles cross-country to a staging area only a mile from Apra Harbor.

We had breakfast in the field and marched along a new macadam road that led to the harbor's facilities. With hundreds of men dressed in full battle gear, we must have made an impressive sight. As our brother services drove past our marching units straddling both sides of the highway, we were met with loud cheering expressions of support that really lifted our morale—at a time when it was extremely welcome.

We boarded a very large troop transport, the *Simon Bolivar*, whose weight must have exceeded 15,000 tons. I happened to be looking down along the ship's rail as we moved away from the dock. As the nose of the ship moved past the dock's massive pilings, the ship barely nudged against the pilings—and before my eyes the pilings splintered like matchsticks.

Iwo Jima

Every marine who fought on this barren island might have justifiably wondered how anyone might have lived there except by coercion, but oddly enough, Iwo Jima had a previous civilian population. The entire group of volcanic islands at the turn of the century was virtually uninhabited. Curiously though, it did have a small civilian population once Japan decided on its expansionist policy when it started pushing south.

In 1877, the mayor of Tokyo visited Iwo Jima. About four years later the island was made a part of the Japanese Empire. Iwo Jima's economy during World War I focused on raising cotton but changed to sugar. In 1915, the island exported over 2,000 kegs, but the economy shifted once more, to making sulfur, produced in a small plant near Motoyama. By 1943, the island had a population of nearly 2,000; about half came from Okinawa. By D-day, all able-bodied men were attached to the military or were laborers, while the women and children were moved to Japan proper.

The shape of Iwo Jima has been compared to a pear or a pork chop. Five miles long and only two and one-half miles wide at its widest point, it covers about eight square miles. Known also as Sulfur

Island, it is practically devoid of vegetation. Mt. Suribachi, on its southern tip, is 560 feet high and the highest point on the island.

Iwo Jima was bombed by our B-24s for seventy-two days and hit with thousands of tons of bombs and naval gunfire. Because of the island's approximate 750 fortifications, they had to be reduced the hard way. Its powerful defenses against our fighting units were held in awe, and its defenders held out against our three Marine divisions for almost forty days. Battle casualties to all three marine divisions were over 26,000 men killed or wounded—an unheard-of loss. The exceptional courage displayed by our forces was reflected by the deep mourning of our nation.

Iwo Jima, strategically located, provided us with an important base as an emergency landing field for our damaged B-29s returning from air raids on Japan. Its fighter strips were also used by P-51s to escort B-29s to Japan, offering important fighter cover for the bombers. Eventually, making forced landings on Iwo's newly lengthened airstrips saved 850 B-29s.

We arrived off the island on February 19, 1945. Our convoy and other ships off the island came under attack from enemy planes that scored some direct hits. The initial landing on the island was made by the Fourth and Fifth Marine Divisions, while our own Third Marine Division was held in reserve. On the 21st, while we waited nervously below decks, the ship's PA system gave the order for our company to form on deck and await the order to climb down the cargo nets into awaiting landing craft.

A sinking and gnawing sensation, along with a real sense of foreboding, permeated our thoughts as we waited intently for the loudspeaker to announce the order for us to go over the side. A commotion ensued around twenty feet to our right. I noticed that one of our men refused to go over the side. This marine fought at Bougainville and was wounded in the Guam campaign. This certainly was not the first time I had witnessed men breaking down under the brutal stress of combat, but our men always showed great sensitivity and compassion for our marine brothers under these conditions. I'm sure that many men thought to themselves that "there but for the grace of God go I." Not breaking faith with our brother battle veterans is the psychological mechanism that makes every infantry unit a truly cohesive force against our adversaries.

With my rifle slung across my back, together with a double pack, I had neglected to fasten my chin strap on my steel helmet. As I raised my leg over the ship's railing, my helmet toppled from my head in a thirty-foot drop toward our men who were in the landing craft below. "Look out!" I bellowed at the top of my lungs. Fortunately, no one was hit by the falling two-and-a-half-pound steel helmet missile. "What in the hell are you doing, Friedman? Trying to get us the purple heart?" "Who, me?" I sheepishly answered.

Stepping down from the cargo net onto the landing craft was treacherous. Because of the large swells, the landing craft would rise and fall some twenty feet, and one misstep was all it took to go into the drink or worse. The choppy sea as we moved toward the beach kept spraying us from the front end of our landing craft. The water was surprisingly cold.

Several warships, including our dive-bombers, were in close to shore, blasting away at Mt. Suribachi. The great palls of smoke practically blanketed the 560-foot-high, steeply walled mountain.

Through Shot and Shell

On the shores of Iwo Jima,
With its blackened sandy beach;
Stood the towering Suribachi,
Whose heights seemed out of reach.

Dug into every craggy seam,
In defense of every yard;
A diehard, skillful enemy,
Made the going very hard.

But in that uphill battle,
Each marine would carve his name;
On the slopes of Suribachi,
In the heaven's hall of fame.
—The author

On the beach the black soft volcanic sand was littered with a variety of heavy equipment, probably struck by enemy artillery fire that was still raking the beach area along with some small arms fire coming from Mt. Suribachi. Our company moved inland quickly, and we dug in just short of Iwo's first airstrip to await further orders. We also heard the sorrowful news that Sergeant John Basilone, a hero of Guadalcanal and a Congressional Medal of Honor winner, was killed in action.

We came under fire around eight p.m. from a 47mm anti-tank gun located on the higher ground just north of us. The enemy no doubt watched us digging in late in the afternoon, and direct fire from a Jap 47mm weapon at our positions was frightening. The shells were exploding only a few feet from us. Fortunately they were not of a higher caliber.

Early next morning, our platoon moved onto the first airstrip itself. While some of our men were drinking coffee, three large mortar shells burst among them, killing and wounding eighteen. As we attended to our wounded, one of our tanks came lumbering by and stopped by our dug-in positions. When the tank's hatch opened, three marines crawled out, all doubled over in agonizing pain. The tank had taken a direct hit from an armor-piercing 77mm shell. Three of us then climbed onto the tank's turret and helped the tank's crew off. By early afternoon, because of the heavy casualties sustained by the First Battalion, our commanding officer was detached from our company and became battalion commander of the First Battalion, Twenty-First Regiment.

Some of the most savage fighting by our First Battalion was now being led by Major Houser. At daybreak the battalion jumped off at 7:30 a.m. and became engaged in a sharp firefight. We were unable to advance until 9:35 a.m., when some of our assault units finally reached the southwest approaches to Iwo's second airstrip.

Finally, after clearing hundreds of enemy pillboxes, our company moved to the edge of the second airstrip. Our third platoon set up two of our 37mm anti-tank guns, which covered the entire approach to the second airstrip. Finally both runways came under our control. We were now able to look north toward the high ground, which was held by elements of the Fourth Marine Division, who had endured intense enemy mortar fire throughout the entire day. On the night of February 26, with our own positions exposed to the enemy, three 90mm shells ripped into us around nine p.m. One of the shells struck one of our vehicles and totally destroyed it. A small piece of shrapnel landed in my foxhole and struck me on the back of my hand. Luckily it caused only a slight cut, which required no attention.

Without any doubt, a stretcher-bearer's exposure to danger in combat has few equals. This unenviable high-risk duty was often designated to our marine brothers in our division's band. However, because of the demoralizing nature of this duty, a system of rotation is normally instituted throughout every unit.

On the morning of February 28, our platoon leader ordered me and another fellow marine to be stretcher-bearers. He told us to follow a northern course along the second airstrip in order to retrieve some marines who were just killed in a firefight and take the bodies to graves registration. While advancing around five hundred yards parallel to the second airstrip, both of us ran right into a firefight some fifty yards or so ahead of us. We quickly dropped to the ground and waited for the automatic weapons fire to subside.

Hot Potato

It's five miles long, just one mile wide,
Few trees or grass it forced to hide;
A smell of sulfur and nights are chilly,
This damn landscape gives me the willies.

Who'd want this turf, it's so grotesque,
Compared to Guam, so picturesque;
Let's forge ahead, and carry on,
To storm the beaches of ol' Nippon.

Its sand is black and steamy too,
Enough to heat our ration stew;
The fiercest battles in one arena,
You guessed right! That's Iwo Jima!
—The author

As we lay there, the soil under us appeared to have an unusual texture. I raised my head slightly and saw in front of me four-foot-high wooden markers with Japanese writing on them. "Christ!" I blurted out, "We're lying in a God-damn Jap cemetery."

When the firing finally subsided, we advanced another fifty to seventy-five yards and came upon two marines killed in the firefight. Both marines were lying facing one another, with their arms locked around the other as in an embrace. "God, almighty!" I exclaimed. "What a sight!" My stretcher partner and I knelt down and had to pry the two marines apart. We then placed them on stretchers. As we lifted the second one, a large wad of bills, wrapped with a rubber band, fell out of his pocket. Although my buddy and I noticed that the roll of money was in large denominations, neither of us had the stomach to pick it up. We just let it lay there.

The long trek back to graves registration was physically exhausting. It became evident as to exactly why the duty of stretcher-bearer had to be rotated among all marine units. I returned to our company, and our lieutenant told us that a call came from Company A. It was being held up by two enemy machine gun nests. They needed a .50 caliber machine gun to penetrate a well-dug-in enemy emplacement near the end of the third Motoyama airstrip. It would take three of us to carry a .50 caliber weapon, together with ammunition for it.

As we approached the third airstrip, some automatic weapons fire was holding up the advance of several marines ahead of us, and I hit the dirt. I cautiously raised my head just above my sandy foxhole. I was amazed to see a combat photographer only ten yards ahead of me; he was attempting to take pictures of the action just ahead of him. However, he was forced, time after time, to duck down as the bullets kicked up the sand around him. This vicious action lasted some ten minutes. The fearless action by the combat photographer, exposing himself to enemy fire, left a lasting impression on me.

Finally we arrived most of the way down the third airstrip. We found A Company dug in just off the strip. Their platoon leader greeted us warmly and asked us to set up our .50 caliber weapon. He pointed out to us the nearby enemy position. We fired several bursts into the approximate enemy position, but no fire was returned. With no enemy fire coming from the hidden machine gun nest, the order was given to the company to advance toward the slopes just beyond the end of the third airstrip.

As I climbed up the higher ground, I came upon a knocked-out Jap tank, which appeared to have been destroyed by a bazooka. All that was showing was the tank's turret. I climbed onto the turret. Not taking any chances, I opened the hatch and dropped a grenade into it as an added precaution. Just ahead of us another fierce firefight was taking place, with heavy automatic fire kicking up the dirt all around me. I was forced to take cover. With the area just forward of us finally secured, the three of us decided to return to our own unit.

As we casually walked alongside the third airstrip toward our company area, we were spotted by a Jap forward observer, who decided to lob four mortar rounds, one at a time. Our casual walk quickly turned into a slow trot. As each mortar round exploded directly in back of us, our pace quickened to a full-blown dash. As I think back, we probably broke the established Olympic record for the 400-yard dash. Fortunately, we were lucky enough to outrun the exploding Jap shells. The Japanese forward observer must have been laughing his ass off as he watched three frightened rabbits literally flying to escape those mortar bursts.

By the first week of March, the enemy had been driven to the most northern sector of Iwo. March 12 was the beginning of final mopping-up operations on the island, as organized resistance in our division's zone of action was reduced to sporadic outbursts. Stubborn resistance, however, was encountered near the crest of the ridge overlooking the seacoast.

The Dreamer

Across this embattled landscape,
As I gaze out towards the sea;
I have a foxhole bird's-eye view,
Of ships anchored on the lee.

> *I'd give anything at this moment,*
> *For some good ole Navy chow;*
> *Instead of these cold rations,*
> *I would not give a starving sow.*
>
> *How I'd love to once change places,*
> *For just one single day;*
> *For the luxury of a shower,*
> *I'd give a whole month's pay.*
> —The author

Our platoon was still dug in at the end of the third Motoyama airstrip, and around eleven a.m., March 14, we were startled to see about a dozen armed Jap soldiers racing across the airstrip. We opened up on them with our small arms weapons, and they all jumped into a large bomb crater smack in the middle of the airstrip. About ten of us ran out and surrounded the bomb crater, waiting for the enemy to come out. Even though we lobbed grenades into the crater, they would toss them out. Finally after fifteen minutes or so, several explosions from the bomb crater went off in succession. As we cautiously approached the rim of the crater, we saw that the enemy had taken their own lives, committing suicide by holding their hand grenades to their chests.

That same afternoon, one of our men spotted one of the enemy running into a small dugout at the very far end of the third airstrip. As we approached the small dugout covered with some wooden planks, we could see the enemy soldier crouched inside. I took up a position behind a very large sandstone boulder some thirty feet from the front end of the dugout, while a few of our men started throwing hand grenades at the rear entrance of the dugout in order to flush the Jap out.

With our grenades exploding at the rear entrance of the dugout, the enemy soldier was forced to come out the front entrance. He crawled out on all fours with his pistol in his hand. With my rifle steadied on top of the boulder, with one of our men just to my left, I fired two rounds simultaneously with him. The Jap soldier dropped in his tracks. I ran over to make sure he was dead. I saw in the rear entrance of the dugout a Samurai sword. I quickly ran around the dugout to retrieve it. Unfortunately I wasn't fast enough because the marines who had lobbed the grenades from the rear of the dugout beat me to it. Although I was too late for that trophy, I did get the Japanese officer's paper money. His personal papers showed that he was a captain in the 112th artillery regiment.

Around two a.m., from my foxhole, I heard a burst of automatic fire just thirty or forty feet to my left, which startled us all. The next morning, a few of us walked over to find out what the shooting was all about. Two enemy soldiers were lying only ten feet from one of our men's foxholes, riddled with bullet holes. They had probably attempted to steal water and rations. The enemy, who was literally starving, desperately tried to infiltrate our lines. They were from some of the remnants holed up in caves in the cliffs that overlooked the beach at Iwo's most northern sector.

With the enemy now attempting to infiltrate our positions for food and water, I made up my mind to remain more alert each night. That same night, at around one or two a.m., I was fully awake. I noticed some faint forms crawling about twenty feet in front of my foxhole. Straining my eyes over my weapon's sight, I placed my finger on the trigger of my B.A.R. However, it was too dark for me to make out if those crawling figures were friendly or enemy. Because I was not sure just who was in my sights, I held my fire. However, I would have been justified in pulling the trigger. It was common knowledge that no one should be out of his foxhole at night, especially with pervasive enemy infiltration almost every night.

In the morning, without revealing what I had witnessed, I asked the marines in the foxhole ahead of mine if they had crawled out during the night. When they had affirmed that it was they who were "just changing foxholes," I blew my stack at them. "You stupid assholes!" I screamed. "Just what in the hell were you thinking of anyway? Do you know, I had you jerks in the sights of my B.A.R.?" I bellowed. I will never know, even to this day, what the repercussions would have been for me had I opened fire. I haven't a clue as to what this burden on my conscience would have been had I killed some of my own buddies.

The same day, while I was scrounging around the area, I found a brand-new pair of Japanese field shoes. Because my own were badly worn, I tried on the new pair, and they fit just perfectly. The only major difference between our field shoes and the Japanese field shoes is that they had hobnails on the soles. So as long as they fit me, I decided to wear them. I never bothered to mention it to the rest of the men. Little did I realize the sensation those Jap shoes would create, and the difficulty I would ultimately encounter trying to keep my balance on the steel deck of the transport ship on the way back to Guam.

Next morning, one of the men noticed the nail imprints left by my hobnailed shoes on the ground all around our foxhole positions. "Hey, look everybody!" yelled one of our men. "There was a Jap walking around our positions last night—will you look at these nail prints?" Being within earshot, I burst out laughing and raised my foot to reveal that I was the culprit. "What in the hell are you doing with Jap shoes, anyway?" one marine asked. "None of your damn business. Now this evens the score for you guys being out of your foxholes the other night!"

On March 16, all organized resistance on Iwo Jima was over, which made it D-day plus twenty-six. However some mopping-up operations were still in effect, which lasted for at least another week. Patrols and ambush parties were sent out on a daily basis to search into bypassed caves and emplacements previously blasted by demolition charges. Japanese-speaking linguists were busily engaged in interrogating prisoners found in caves that had been sealed during the fighting.

The incredible courage, skill, and unconquerable determination of every man who fought there won the battle for Iwo Jima. No conceivable defense by the enemy, although so numerous on Iwo, would stop us. From the standpoint of the extremely limited size of the battlefield, compared to the size of the forces engaged, there are probably few battles in history that surpass Iwo Jima in magnitude and fury. On eight square miles of sand and rock, 85,000 marines and 24,000 Japanese fought to the death. Our own Third Marine Division's cost was 5,569 casualties, of which 1,131 were killed.

In the words of our division's commanding officer, General Erskine, "Only the accumulated praise of time will pay proper tribute to our valiant dead. Long after those who lament their immediate loss are themselves dead, these men will be mourned by the Nation. Victory was never in doubt; only its cost was!"

On March 22, when we left the area of Motoyama Airstrip Three, our platoon made its way back to the first airstrip to await the arrival of transport ships to take us back to Guam. With the campaign over, it wasn't necessary for us to dig any more foxholes. The first thing we did was to clean our filthy bodies from the grime of over a month's fighting. Inasmuch as fresh water was so scarce, all we could do was take one of those proverbial "whore's baths," as we called them. We were allowed only one helmet of fresh water. We used a small amount of it in order to lather up. What remained in the steel helmet we used to rinse ourselves off. Water was extremely scarce inasmuch as all of the drinking water on the island had to come from the ships anchored offshore.

Being in close proximity to the first airstrip, one of our favorite pastimes was to visit the damaged B-29s parked on the airfield. Those were the planes that were not capable of making it back to Guam or Saipan from their raids on Japan. Some were so badly shot up that it was a miracle they managed to bring the plane and crew back. It became obvious to us how important this island was to our air force. With Iwo Jima now in our hands, it was clear how the island was able to save over eight hundred B-29s, together with their irreplaceable crews, from a watery grave.

The bantering sessions we marines had with the bombers' crews while exchanging war stories was exciting, and their gratitude toward us marines was highly appreciated. Some of the men traded Japanese souvenirs for their easy-to-get bottles of whiskey.

Bless Them All!

Bless them all! Bless them all!
The long, the short, and the tall.
There'll be no promotion,
This side of the ocean,
So cheer up, my lads, bless them all.

So we're saying goodbye to them all,
As back to our foxholes we crawl,
There'll be no promotion,
This side of the ocean,
So cheer up, Gyrenes, bless them all.
—The author

At five a.m. on March 24, all living hell broke loose along the opposite coastline. Approximately one hundred fifty Japs in full combat gear had worked their way from their caves at the most northern end of Iwo and made it to the edge of the first airstrip. They attacked the air force crews who were still asleep in their cots. Several of the air force men were killed. Completely caught by surprise, our units engaged the do-or-die Jap troops in some of the fiercest fighting to date. It wasn't until late morning that all one hundred fifty were annihilated.

There seemed to be an irrepressible mind-set that emanated from our battle-seasoned men during the last few days of the fighting on Iwo. This action, for many of us, was our third campaign. What seemingly became so paramount in the minds of we "old-timers" was simply how to survive the last few days of the campaign. With two years overseas and two previous campaigns, our thoughts would reflect that on the field of battle, nothing is improbable.

Those original adrenaline surges we all possessed so many months ago had just about dissipated. Now, with only a few days left in the fighting, some had singularly devised a way of trying to stay alive and in one piece. If there was one luxury that frontline soldiers possessed, it was the luxury of reflective contemplation. With anxious, somber expressions on the faces of the men, just one thought permeated our minds: No more heroics ... we paid our dues!

In relating the many events of my three island campaigns, I have placed much of the emphasis on our frontline actions. Unfortunately, recognition of our artillery, engineers, pioneers, Seabees, and the service troops remained in the background, yet it was they who also had to bear, endure, and carry out the extremely difficult and thankless tasks so important in every military campaign.

Our company boarded ship on March 27. After some thirty-five days on that God-forsaken island, we arrived back on Guam April 1, 1945, with an announcement playing over the ship's loudspeaker that the Okinawa landing had taken place by the

First and Sixth Marine Divisions, with strong support by units of the Eighth Army.

We were surprised upon our arrival back at our old campsite that some of our units had been evicted by new replacements, including our company living quarters. In an announcement at a company formation, we were informed that we "old-timers" would be sent back to the states in ten days or so.

One morning at a company formation, the new replacements platoon leader announced the day's assignment for the new men. He then turned to us and said, "You men have it made!" And put us on a working party detail.

After our three campaigns and almost twenty-seven months overseas, this ninety-day wonder had the audacity to tell us, "You have it made!" He was probably in high school when we all left for overseas duty. And what's more is the fact that the very ground he stood on was paid for in blood by so many of our men. On the working detail, in the bantering that went on among us, over and over again, someone would invariably with a heavy dose of sarcasm yell out, "Say, Friedman, you have it made!" In turn, I would turn to the marine standing nearby and say, "Hey, Wilson! Did you know that you have it made?" This went on and on, but those humorous retorts helped to relieve our pent-up anger.

The big day finally arrived. On April 13, 1945, about fifty-four of us—out of our original group of some 224 men—boarded trucks that took us to Apra Harbor. While our vehicles were awaiting orders to move out, the news came over the company loudspeaker that President Roosevelt had died. Every man was deeply saddened by the enormous loss of our wartime commander in chief.

We were pleasantly surprised to hear that we would return home on the *Hollandia*, a small escort aircraft carrier that was primarily used to ferry fighter planes from the states to Guam.

The hangar deck was set up with row upon row of sleeping cots. But most important, we could not believe the great navy food and the ship's stores we had been given access to. The ship's stores included among many other things a soda fountain and genuine ice cream. We started to act like young children in a candy store. We literally had to pinch ourselves to believe that this was actually happening.

Most of the men would spend hours on the ship's flight deck exercising and sunbathing. The trip home would take seventeen days, with a one-day stopover at Pearl Harbor to pick up many marines that had been wounded on Iwo Jima. I can vividly remember, as our ship pulled into the harbor, how solemn and quiet we stood on the ship's deck. We realized that this was where the war started over three years ago. Pearl Harbor now showed very little of the original damage that was leveled upon it by the Japanese attack.

On May 1, 1945, our ship pulled into the harbor at North Island, California, and we boarded buses that took us to the marine barracks at San Diego. As our buses drove across its flat well-manicured grounds, we could not help but take notice of hundreds of marine recruits being drilled. This for us certainly brought back memories. We arrived about noon and headed to the dining room for lunch. We acted like starved vultures. Whoever first grabbed the pitchers of milk guzzled down at least two or three glasses full before relinquishing them.

It would take at least a week before the necessary paperwork, physicals, and issuance of new clothes and uniforms. At the post exchange, the men purchased the necessary accoutrements and trappings with which we would adorn our dress uniforms. The campaign ribbons our Third Marine Division had earned were the Navy Commendation, the Presidential Unit Citation, and the Asiatic Pacific Ribbon with four battle stars. Also available were ribbons for the Purple Heart, Bronze Star, and Silver Star for those men who had earned them. We were surprised to learn that our fourth battle star was for the Bougainville campaign. It seems the fourth star was earned because on the eighth day of the campaign, as I understand it, the enemy landed seventeen barges of troops behind our lines; the fourth battle star was consequently awarded the division for the defense and occupation of Bougainville.

Having received our thirty-day furlough papers, most of the men left San Diego for the East Coast. For those men who lived on the West Coast, other types of transportation was afforded. After five days by train, we finally arrived in Washington, D.C. We changed trains once more for the northeast. I arrived in New York's Pennsylvania Station with a platoon buddy who was from New York City, and we decided to walk the ten blocks to Broadway and 42nd Street. Much to our surprise, a small statue of the raising of our flag on Iwo Jima was installed in the center island that divided Broadway and Seventh Avenue.

As we stood quietly and solemnly before the statute, alongside several civilian onlookers, two members of the Navy Shore Patrol approached us. My buddy, having enlisted at the ripe old age of seventeen and still looking like a high school teenager, naturally attracted the attention of the shore patrol, especially with our uniforms adorned with four battle stars. The Shore Patrol respectfully asked to see our furlough papers. Naturally we obliged unhesitatingly. With our thirty-day leave papers in order, the two SP's thanked us with a friendly handshake and wandered off.

Gotcha

Arriving home on furlough leave;
One lovely summer's day,
The Shore Patrol would stop me,
For questions, they would say.

"You look so young in uniform,
We've seen this twice before,
And wearing several battle stars,
How did you earn all four?"

"This star's for Iwo Jima,
And this one is for Guam,
The other two for Bougainville,"
Speaking slow and calm.

"Your story is very interesting,"
The two S.P.'s would say,
"Your papers are in order, sir,
You have a real nice day."
—The author

We both took the subway home, and during the ride we were met by curious stares from the train's passengers. Their curiosity, however, was never aroused enough to ask us any questions. My buddy's train took him to the Washington Heights section in Manhattan, while I continued up to the Bronx.

I was able to stay at my aunt's apartment for a week. The family was overjoyed at my return, which made my stay very comfortable. My dad, who had come to New York from New Jersey, took one look at me and remarked, "Joe, you don't look very well!" I was somewhat startled by his remark. The only way I thought I could calm him was to reply that "it was only about eight weeks ago that I was on Iwo Jima." I also tried to put on some more weight in order to satisfy him.

My dad and I returned to Flemington, New Jersey, by train. I visited our hometown newspaper and was quizzed extensively by the publisher, who had also informed me that another marine was in town on furlough who likewise was in the Third Marine Division. Without hesitation, I visited this marine's home and was fortunate to find him. I knew him from high school but did not realize that he was in the same division as I. Together we spent many hours talking with each other about our experiences. In addition, I had the pleasant opportunity to meet his wonderful family. Incidentally, the publisher of our local newspaper gave me a wonderful write-up, and it seemed as though as I walked around town everyone was eager to shake my hand.

My thirty-day leave was quickly nearing its end, and I returned to New York City and stayed at my aunt's apartment for the remaining few days. My furlough orders indicated that I was to report to the Portsmouth Naval Prison in Portsmouth, New Hampshire, for duty with the small marine detachment. Most of the prisoners at this naval prison were there for very serious offenses. It usually required a general court-martial in order to be sentenced there. I found the duty at the prison great, with one day on and two days off. The local beaches seemed to be a magnet for girls from the surrounding cities and towns. With the summer in full swing, it appeared as if a new crop of women arrived at this beautiful resort area every week.

Inasmuch as it was now during the heart of the summer, I decided to take in one of the local beaches for what I thought would be a nice cool dip in the ocean. However, much to my surprise, the ocean water was extremely cold, so I could not venture any deeper than my ankles. Amazingly, this was in July.

For some reason, marines at the naval prison's detachment rarely wore their campaign ribbons on liberty. I never once investigated as to why, but the local town's people in Portsmouth all knew that the marines doing duty in the navy yard and at the prison were all veterans of the Pacific campaigns.

One of the semiweekly rituals for me was to attend the dances at the local beach casino, which overlooked the beautiful Atlantic Ocean beach. It was in the height of the summer; the dress code for us was plain summer khaki. On one particular evening while standing just off the dance floor, as I tried to make up my mind as to which gal to ask for a dance, an army air force captain brushed quickly by me in his dress uniform bedecked with a chestful of campaign ribbons.

Apparently in an attempt to impress the girl he was with, he quickly spun around, and standing directly in front of me with his face up close to mine, he brusquely ordered that I tuck in my tie. Taken aback slightly, but in full control, I politely responded, "Sorry, captain, but it is against Marine Corps regulations for us to tuck in our field scarves, sir!" Obviously confused, he looked me up and down and walked away a little embarrassed. As an afterthought, had I worn my campaign ribbons, the incident probably would never have occurred.

One of our duties at the naval prison was to take small groups of prisoners on work details just outside the prison's gates. On one of those details, one of the prisoners turned to me and asked, "Say, pal—if I were to make a run for it, would you shoot me?" Without hesitation I responded, "Why not try it and find out for yourself?" That response ended the conversation. The other prisoners also took their cue from my firm reply.

The naval prison's grounds were surrounded by tall concrete towers that overlooked the bay. Standing duty one lovely day on one of the towers, which looked toward the sea, I was stunned by a sight that made be disbelieve my own eyes. I saw a submarine, not too far from us, riding on the surface and approaching the navy yard. The conning tower of the sub had the numerals U505. I stared in disbelief and remarked to myself, "That's a German sub!" I immediately phoned the sergeant of the guard and yelled into the phone, "Hey, sarge! There's a German submarine approaching on the surface of the ocean, and it's coming toward us!" "Calm down, Friedman! That's a German sub captured by our navy last year, so just relax!"

Arriving in New York City for the weekend and upon leaving Grand Central Station, I could see smoke billowing from the Empire State Building. "What happened?" I asked the first person who passed by. "Didn't you hear?" the stranger replied. "A B-25 bomber crashed into the Empire State Building!"

As I rode the subways to get around New York City, I could not help feeling a little self-conscious because of the curious stares from some of the subway passengers. The sight of a marine in the summer of 1945 with so many of our armed forces still overseas seemed to arouse their curiosity, but nobody questioned me.

At the time that I was on leave, I was quite thin. In an attempt to put on a little more weight, I went to one of the neighborhood ice cream stores and ordered a chocolate milkshake. After a few sips, I remarked to the proprietor that the malted was a little weak and it probably needed some additional malt powder. "Don't you know there's a war on?" he curtly responded. I pointed to my campaign ribbons and quickly snapped back, "You see these battle stars—just where in the hell do you think I got them? You jerk! You can take the rest of this watery milkshake and shove it!" I retorted as I walked out of the store.

The summer days of 1945 seemed to fly by so quickly, and before I knew it, Japan had announced to the world that it would accept the Allied terms for surrender. On August 14 the city of Portsmouth announced it would be having a celebration commemorating the event that evening. I would have loved to attend, but unfortunately for me, I caught guard duty at the main gate of the prison. I would miss the festivities. As I watched so many of the marines from the detachment leaving on liberty that evening, it certainly was a low point for me.

When the total surrender of Japan was declared on September 2, 1945, a point system was instituted whereby those who had amassed a total of at least eighty-five points would have the first opportunity to request a discharge. Inasmuch as I had eighty-six points and met all the requirements for discharge, a Red Cross official interviewed me. One of the questions during my interview was whether I was entitled to any pension. Since I was hospitalized twice on Guadalcanal for malaria with a strong possibility of future occurrences, I asked the interviewer if my malaria rated a pension. The official informed me that it would take at least six weeks for them to check my service medical records. I was anxious to return to civilian life, and I did not want to stay in the service any longer. I decided to decline filling out the necessary forms for a pension.

On October 5, 1945, I received my honorable discharge papers from the marines. I also received my mustering-out pay, with an allowance given me for the train ride to New York City. It would be convenient for me to stay at my aunt's apartment and to apply at the Veterans Administration for veteran's benefits. One of the immediate benefits was a weekly stipend of twenty dollars a week, which would last for fifty-two weeks or until one found employment.

Every discharged veteran was allowed to wear his uniform for thirty days after being discharged. One easy way to tell a discharged veteran was a small golden eagle that was worn on the right-hand side of his uniform. After three weeks, I decided to purchase civilian clothes and stopped wearing the uniform. During my thirty-day furlough, I became reacquainted with some of the guys I knew before the war. They were still in uniform, though, and fortunately for them they had not served overseas.

One day we all decided to visit the Times Square area. With me in my civilian clothes and they in uniform, I felt like a fish out of water. We stopped at an open bar for a beer or two. My two uniformed friends struck up a friendly conversation with the bartender, who seemed naturally curious listening to our stories. However, any attempt to inject myself into the conversation was rebuffed so that I could not even get a word in edgewise. It immediately occurred to me that had I worn my uniform, no doubt I would have received the same courtesy and attention that my uniformed pals received.

With a few days left of my furlough, I decided to visit my cousin Dan. He reminded me that the jobs I was contemplating provided no future. Dan held a job in a commercial print shop and had me visit him the next working day. One of the more interesting jobs he was doing was setting type on a casting machine called a Linotype. When I asked him how much he was being paid, I was impressed.

"Why don't you use your GI Bill and go to printing school?" he suggested. I thought about the idea for a few days and decided to take his advice. I registered at the New York School of Printing under the GI Bill of Rights, and a better choice—thanks to my cousin—was never made. After five years as an apprentice, I finally became a journeyman printer and applied for my union card.

In 1983, my wife started to show the first signs of Parkinson's disease. We then moved to Florida where, as her caregiver, I would be in a better position to provide her with one-on-one attention. However, as her condition deteriorated, the job of caring for her became physically and emotionally overwhelming for me. In order to save my own health, I was compelled to commit her to a nursing home.

Recall to Arms

Things sure get lonely around this old house.
The children have gone, including my spouse;
Faded memories of comrades of past yesteryears,
I dwell on those great times I hold very dear.
Many years have gone by, I could not prevent,
With memories of battles, such momentous events.

So if this sounds foolish, don't look so aghast,
If I had my druthers, I'd return in a flash.
—The author

Return to Guam

In the spring of 1994, with the fiftieth anniversary of the Guam landings approaching, I made some inquiries and found that the Military Historical Tours, the country's premier coordinator of military tour programs, was initiating a reunion to honor the veterans of the Guam campaign. This reunion would take place on Guam from July 16 to 21, 1994. I immediately contacted Military Historical Tours, and a registration form was mailed to me.

I left Ft. Lauderdale Airport on Continental Airlines on July 14. We made stops at Houston, Texas, and Los Angeles, California, then went on to Hawaii the next day. Transferring to another plane, we left Hawaii with about one hundred marine veterans. All told, approximately 1,100 veterans would make the return trip to Guam on other flights. The distance from Hawaii to Guam is 3,300 miles; the flight took us seven and one-half hours. Many returning veterans were traveling with their wives, which made the trip warm and friendly in an atmosphere of some remarkably nostalgic incidents.

During the flight from Hawaii to Guam, the aircraft's captain invited us to come forward into the plane's cockpit, where he would explain how the aircraft's complicated systems worked.

The pilot asked me about some of my own experiences during the Guam campaign and was so taken with some of my combat incidents that he called the stewardess and told her to give me a seat in first class. Needless to say, I was overwhelmed by the captain's generous offer.

The pilot banked the aircraft as we approached the island, which gave us a clear view of the high steep cliffs jutting up from the ocean. We could not have been more than 1,500 feet high, and the view was spectacular. Once we landed, a long red carpet was spread out on the tarmac. A cordon of high-ranking officers were lined up on each side. They saluted us as we passed through them on the way to the receiving area. Under a large canopy set up with hundreds of chairs, Governor Ada of Guam made the official welcoming speech as many other dignitaries looked on.

Our bus ride to the hotel took only five minutes, and surprisingly the accommodations were excellent. Unfortunately, my roommate had a severe case of asthma, and every so often had to hook himself up to an oxygen machine; he was great company nevertheless. Breakfast each morning at the hotel was buffet style, with a large variety of food choices. By nine a.m. we boarded buses, and the first visit on our itinerary was the landing beach at Asan Point.

It was here, some fifty years ago, that we hit the beach. I must have practically retraced my footsteps, which were made so many years before. Somehow, one gets the feeling of a surrealist impression that is very difficult to interpret in a coherent fashion. As we continued to take in the beach area, many TV cameras and newspaper reporters were interspersed through the large gathering. I was approached by one of the TV cameramen, who asked me many questions about my participation in the landing.

As I pointed to the beach area some fifty yards or so away, I told them that was exactly where I had waded ashore in the first few minutes of the landing. Then I turned toward the Chonito Hills and pointed to an area that stood out in the bright morning sunlight. Pointing to the approximate sector I had dug in during that banzai attack, I gave the TV reporters a full accounting of the action that took place during that fateful night some fifty years before. All was said with the TV camera grinding away. At one point, Governor Ada came over. He was very interested in my action analysis and continued asking me questions as to what took place on Fonte Ridge during the early morning attack. I was surprised how little the governor knew about the details of that early morning battle on Fonte Ridge. I must have been stopped at least three or four more times by newspaper reporters with their inquisitive, penetrating questions, and I eagerly obliged them all.

The War Lover

The heartbeat will quicken,
And it stirs the soul;
Remembering the yesteryears,
When we all played a role;
In America's answer to engage her foes,
With the smell of gunpowder,
wafting by our nose.

Civilian life over many years,
Had its ups and downs, along with tears;
But we'll admit to one and all in prose,
The joy of gunpowder, wafting past the nose.

It may sound foolish now, and yet,
Ask any veteran and you'll likely get,
A familiar answer from a gestured pose,
How they loved the gunpowder,
Wafting past their nose.
—The author

At Asan Point itself, hundreds of chairs were set up in a parklike area, with a marine band and marine drill team giving a splendid display of close order drill. The entire area became silent when from the podium, the governor and many of the island's dignitaries, which included our own marine corps commandant, gave stirring speeches honoring all the veterans who had participated in the invasion. Finally, a large, beautiful granite monument, emblazoned with the Third Marine Division's three-cornered emblem, was unveiled. It was a moving sight for us veterans and choked us up considerably.

By eleven a.m. we boarded our buses for the landing beaches used by the Marine First Provisional Brigade and the Army's Seventy-Seventh Division. Once again, memorial services were held, which included a memorial for the other branches of our armed services whose men were killed in action. From there we visited a war museum that had several displays of enemy equipment and Japanese uniforms. The walls of the museum were studded with dozens of pictures.

As I stood there entirely engrossed, I heard a voice next to me giving his wife an explanation of a display. We both turned toward each other simultaneously. The recognition was instantaneous. The greeting toward each other after so many years was unbelievable. I thought for a moment that this Marine buddy, whom I instantly recognized, almost forgot for a moment that he had a wife, but he regained his composure. We both made sure to share our room numbers, lest we become separated during the rest of the guided tour.

Back at the hotel that evening, he called and we made sure to meet during the dinner hour to talk over old times. During dinner, he informed me there was another member staying at the hotel who just happened to be in my own third platoon. Scanning around the dining room, we spotted him at a nearby table with his wife. After so many years, I could still recognize him. Greeting me with much enthusiasm, we both talked about our postwar lives. He remembered that it was I who was with him on the bazooka team when we lost the bazooka's batteries during that ill-fated attempt to knock out a Jap 77mm weapon. "Please," I begged, "don't remind me of that miserable experience." I was absolutely amazed with the clarity and his memory of the incident.

The next day we attended the "Golden Salute!" honoring us so-called "liberators" in a large park complex, where Governor Ada and other officials praised us in their speeches. A lovely group of children sang in choir form, which was very colorful and quite moving. The unveiling of two statues also was part of the ceremonies. One statue honored the people of Guam for their brave acts of courage displayed during the Japanese occupation. In addition, there was a statue of marines on patrol accompanied by scouts from Guam's civilian militia. Both statues were very emotional for me.

The modern Guam, with its luxurious hotels, modern roads, and industry, was a far cry from the past. Late in the afternoon, we were invited to go aboard the carrier USS *Belleau Wood* for an evening of entertainment, which included a wonderful buffet dinner on the hangar deck. An excellent marine drill team gave us a snappy display on the ship's flight deck of close order drill. The navy sailors were very hospitable and gave us a complete tour of the modern carrier. With fine young men like these, our country's military is in excellent hands.

On the fourth and final day, one of the tour guides asked if any of us wanted to tour the frontlines on Fonte Ridge. Turning to me, the guide mentioned that he only had three men that wanted to go. I must have had a hundred nightmares over the years, and I told the guide that I felt quite nervous about returning to the area where the banzai attack took place. Anyway, still filled with trepidation, I agreed to go along.

The ride to the top of the Chonito Hills took about ten minutes. As we covered the very ground where the banzai charge took place, I must have been only a few feet from where I originally lay over fifty years ago. The steep drop from the edge of the cliff was only some ten feet from my original foxhole. To say that I was nervous as I looked over the very spot, which hardly changed, would be an understatement. My stomach became a little queasy. No wonder I remained fairly solemn on the way back to the hotel.

On July 22, 1994, our wonderful four-day "Golden Salute" visit ended, and we departed for the airport at about ten a.m. for Hawaii and went home. The return back to Guam after fifty years for me meant more than words could possibly convey. Guam's wonderful warm and friendly people will always remain close to my heart, along with some of the most wonderful memories of my life.

Afterword

After more than six decades, I can still see with clarity in my mind's eye the many innocent youthful faces of all the brave warriors we lost in battle. For me at least, their youthful, innocent faces will forever remain young and handsome. With the eternal spirit of comradeship, I will continue to dedicate myself to their revered memory.

One of the several mementos I brought back from the Pacific was the original set of my dog tags. One of the more unusual incidents I was confronted with was about my dog tags. The incident happened while we were in New Zealand. Before leaving that charming country, we were told to renew our old dog tags for new ones and had to give the pertinent information to our company corpsman. As every serviceman is aware, one's name, serial number, blood type, and religious affiliation are stamped onto the dog tags. When the company corpsman asked what religious affiliation to put on my dog tags, such as "C" for Catholic, "P" for Protestant, or "H" for Hebrew, he refused to believe that I was of the Jewish faith. Without informing me, the corpsman, of his own volition, had the letter "P" stamped onto my dog tags, and throughout the entire war it remained a fait accompli.

Postscript

And when we reach the gates of heaven,
To St. Peter we shall tell;
One more marine reporting, Sir,
We served our time in hell.
—The author

Perspectives

I have always believed, and have consistently maintained, that most all war veterans who have experienced the ravages of close combat want in some way to have their personal experiences either heard about or written about. To readers fortunate enough to not have to relive over and over again the mental scars that battle creates, I would humbly suggest it is practically impossible to comprehend the lingering and latent stress created from its consequences. Battle daily subjects the individual to being caught up by the flux of events, wherein the individual has practically no control in managing his or her own fate. The sting of battle creates its own conditions, making no distinction as to who lives or dies.

Without any doubt, I am sure that most men in their respective units made their own personal analysis to help choose those men they wanted to be around in combat when crisis decisions were made ... sort of an insurance policy. It was no secret as to who the best marksmen were and whom could be relied upon under fire to remain cool, calm, and collected—a reputation, I might add, fortunately attained by many men.

There have been situations occasionally when a soldier's own instincts in battle may give that individual a greater chance for survival. As an example, take an ordinary buck private who has been in action for many weeks with a proven record of knowing how to lead. This soldier could have better instincts under fire than those of an officer with very limited battle experience. There were times when our officers with much less combat experience would rely on the judgment of their platoon sergeants during the ebb and flow in a series of firefights with the enemy. Therefore, it goes without saying that in the final analysis, intestinal fortitude along with experience in combat is a formula that should never be dismissed in making those important decisions in the selection of unit leadership.

I am convinced that many of our battle successes against our formidable Japanese adversaries were because of our well-planned and thorough training program. The marine corps' steadfast commitment to our training made it absolutely imperative that every marine trained would completely comprehend a variety of weapons and their usage. The one common denominator in so many of the actions we engaged in was the unbending confidence we had in every marine's ability to literally hit, with a high degree of consistency, any target in our weapons' sights.

It must have been one of the more demoralizing aspects for the enemy, forced to sustain so many casualties from the deadly accuracy of our small arms weapons alone. It is no wonder that the enemy took such pains to conceal and camouflage themselves in an effort to avoid becoming battle statistics.

As for the Japanese soldier's reputation in combat against us, there is little doubt that our enemy was tenacious, cunning, and highly motivated. Japanese bravery in actions against us remains positively legendary, but they also had a reputation for treachery. In one of our indoctrination classes, our officers told us of an incident during the Guadalcanal campaign.

Our marine officer related the incident of a small marine patrol that encountered three enemy soldiers with their arms raised in surrender. As the marine patrol attempted to take them prisoner, the first Japanese soldier bent over quickly, which revealed an automatic weapon strapped to his back. The second enemy soldier of their three-man patrol quickly opened fire and cut down, without the slightest warning, our marine patrol. From then on, we knew the enemy had no compunction about pulling dirty stunts like that, making us extremely cautious in any similar future encounter. Enemy nighttime infiltration to probe any weaknesses in our frontline positions was a common practice, and we all had to be extremely alert against these tactics.

As for us, we often witnessed and discussed Japanese tenacity. The enemy had an amazing capacity to withstand over and over again our murderous preliminary artillery bombardments and air strikes against their positions. Believing that nothing could possibly survive our heavy bombardments, we were stunned when we were met by the enemy's withering counterfire once we attacked their strongpoints. The counterfire had a demoralizing effect on our psyche, as we were often more than a little bewildered just how the enemy could withstand that devastating punishment.

It became obvious to many of us that the Japanese ancient chivalric warrior's code "Bushido" was what helped so many enemy soldiers hold out all those years in their island jungle habitats. Their ability to sustain themselves under the most primitive living conditions so long was why I found the warrior's code so fascinating. The Bushido Code requires, among many other tenets, a martial spirit, including athletic and military skills as well as fearlessly facing the enemy in battle. It also held that the supreme honor was to serve one's emperor unto death. I shudder to contemplate the carnage our armed forces might have had to sustain if our military brass had to follow through with their proposed invasion on the Japanese home islands in November 1945.

Of primary importance is to give the reader an intelligible accounting by rendering in this book's dialogue a mental-visual picture. Hopefully it is sustained by uncomplicated narratives, which reveal how our frontline soldiers were able to respond under the enormous pressures of combat as they continually engaged a dedicated, cunning, and resourceful adversary.

Our bloodlust for the hated enemy was insatiable and very often helped us to overcome our own fears during an engagement. At no time during the entire war did our hatred change or even diminish. While this may sound a little ghoulish, the sight of the enemy dead helped to destroy a prevalent contemporary myth of Japanese invincibility, thus instilling in our fighting units a much higher degree of self-confidence.

I sincerely believe that what the reader understands and assimilates may be construed as truthful. From an admitted partisan viewpoint, I earnestly hope that our combat veterans will look favorably upon this account. I welcome their thoughts and opinions because I humbly suggest that only they have the moral justification for a critical analysis.

It would not be that unusual nor that uncommon for our veterans who have experienced actual combat to forthrightly give similar assessments about the same engagement—or to make a different assessment and come to other conclusions in their interpretations. But any hypothesis must be scrupulously examined for its intellectual validity. I would humbly add that he who has paid the piper should call the tunes. It is practically impossible to remember the dozens of daily hostile predicaments we were confronted with in the day-to-day routine of a campaign. Unfortunately, we marines were not permitted to keep a diary, although a few men did so secretly and I am sorry that I did not.

Even though I still possess most of the letters I wrote home, which the family saved for me, they were not very informative because of the strict censorship. I am very pleased that so many action incidents in this book's narrative have remained so indelibly imprinted in my mind. Without realizing it, as I read over the manuscript in order to rephrase many of the narratives, I still get a good feeling when my thoughts permit me to relive the more happy moments. Of course, the dark and sinister events also have a needed purpose, and it is important for me not to eschew those passages because they have given me the added resolve of not forgetting the bravest of deeds by the men I fought with. One regret is that I am unable to express in words more succinctly and profoundly the courage of our brave warriors.

The vignettes of close combat and abundant related incidents during and in between several smaller engagement sequences allude to just how tenuous the life of an infantryman can be. Being absolutely circumspect when the chips are down is a key element for staying in one piece. I suppose there will always be those who will be fascinated by the exciting action details written and told by those who have lived through them and are anxious to share their wartime experiences for the sake of posterity. With millions of individual personal experiences in actions never before told or heard about, it is vital and indispensable, from a historical perspective, that articles and books continue to flow to the masses so that readers can try to understand just how brutal and senseless wars can be. There is no way that I wish to glorify my own wartime experiences and the many personal tragedies that even today, decades later, still continue to stir emotions that are almost impossible to comprehend.

With deserved high praise and full acknowledgment for our brother services, it remains an undeniable fact that their dedication and consistent valor in armed combat remains strikingly obvious. Nevertheless, with an understandable sense of pride, I want to pay deserved homage to our own line company units for having sustained for weeks and months on end frontline duty. We were constantly soaked from daily torrents of rain while enduring the daily misery of living in muddy foxholes, surviving countless nights with very little sleep and on slim rations, and repulsing frequent enemy night assaults against our weakened positions. We always felt blessed for having witnessed another morning's sunrise.

When constructing any fair and impartial examination into our civilian prewar backgrounds, one must be totally objective by taking into account the physical and psychological factors that sustained so many of our men under these protracted, undeniably degrading living conditions. Week after week our men endured horrendous conditions in those swampy insect-infected jungles throughout the Pacific theater. I, for one, am convinced that I owe my physical condition due to the heavy manual labor I did on our farm before the war. For example, having survived two malaria attacks on Guadalcanal in 1943 and being hospitalized on Guam with dengue fever and dysentery simultaneously, my prewar background on our farm gave me the strength and helped me survive those serious illnesses while so many others did not.

Arriving at forward positions by the end of the second day on Bougainville, our lieutenant happened to notice how dexterous I was swinging an ax as I chopped away at the coconut logs I was using to cover my foxhole with. Naturally, the lieutenant could not possibly know the earlier years I spent on our farm cutting down all those trees for firewood. As I chopped away at the logs in a real steamy, agitated mood, with oceans of sweat and grime pouring from me, the lieutenant complimented me on my proficiency with the ax and asked, "Hey, Friedman, did ya'll make Pfc yet?" Unhesitatingly, without thoughtfully measuring my response, I blurted out, "You know fuckin' aye well I'm still a private, *sir!*"

For whatever reason, but fortunately for me, the lieutenant took no exception from my outburst. I am certain he knew how many of us already had well over a year of military service with nine months already spent overseas without receiving one lousy stripe. It is also noteworthy that, and one might consider speculating why, our officers, especially in combat, were less prone to take disciplinary action against enlisted men. There is a rational explanation as to why, but I leave it up to the reader's imagination to ponder. Our tough marine units were always capable of doing the best when caught up in very precarious situations. The fighting spirit of the marine corps' line units, with their forge-ahead tactics against heavily entrenched enemy positions during our island campaigns, was nothing more than sheer defiance in the face of a tenacious, formidable adversary. Not surprisingly, in the annals of warfare, America's fighting men fought with the highest tradition of dedication and bravery. The many calamities in the maelstrom of events during battle can only be described as savage and yet sometimes serene.

I know I speak for every marine in paying homage to our clergy, who made it their mission to alleviate our understandable fears. Their youthful appearance often belied their station within our ranks. Were it not for the small golden cross affixed to the collar of their fatigues, the chaplains would hardly be recognized as they quietly made their rounds among our units on the frontlines. They talked, listened, and inspired our youthful fighters.

Our clergy carried no sidearms for their protection, and the men looked upon the "padres" as saintly with their quiet, dignified manner. "Say, padre," was a constant refrain from the men, "How soon are we going stateside?" These questions were especially from those of us who were already overseas nearly two years.

Psychological Profile

Presented in one of several orientation sessions given to us by our officers on Guadalcanal, a captured Japanese Army manual gave a psychological profile of the American Soldier. It described America's fighting men as not warlike, but if they were aroused into action, they would be formidable adversaries. The manual went on to describe how well we did in technical and mechanical aspects under battlefield situations. Our youths, it revealed, were also very proficient in motor skills and quite knowledgeable in all aspects of machinery.

The Japanese writers of this manual did not seem to understand or even comprehend that our generation was raised in the crucible of a severe depression, when America's young people had to live on barely one or two skimpy meals daily. The simple niceties we now enjoy did not exist for us back then.

One or two pairs of pants and a few shirts were all we had, and yet our mothers meticulously kept us neat and clean for school. So often, one could see a mother bringing a little extra food to school to feed another poor child along with her own. Life was very difficult, and with this background of privation, America's servicemen in World War II knew tough times years before entering military service.

Japanese warlords, no doubt, never took into account all of these factors. Psychologically, we were toughened very early to withstand the rigors we would eventually meet in that cauldron of sustained land warfare.

Final Thoughts

Throughout history many cultures—Alexander the Great, Rome under the Caesars, Spain, England, Nazi Germany—have sought world hegemony for themselves in a military fashion. Japan's expansionist policies started with the defeat of Czarist Russian forces on land and sea in the Sino-Japanese war of 1904–05. With the ignominious defeat of a western power, the rising sun never shown more brightly.

With its population burgeoning and very limited natural resources of its own, Japan embarked on an aggressive war westward into the heart of the Asian continent, proclaiming its expansion as the Greater East Asia Co-Prosperity Sphere.

The United States was hampered by the Washington Conference for Arms Limitation in 1921–22 when it attempted to stall Japan's military expansion in the Pacific. Under protection of a previous naval treaty with England signed at the turn of the century, Japan laid claim to the many islands taken from Germany after World War I. By fortifying these islands that lay north of Micronesia, they formed a defensive circle that extended as a concentric outer ring that would neutralize any United States advance in the Pacific.

The United States, constrained by the 1921–22 Naval Treaty, was effectively blocked from fortifying Guam, Wake Island, and the Philippines. Not wishing to antagonize Japan, the United States lost the initiative. However, the United States ultimately changed its position and in 1939 asked Congress to appropriate five million dollars to the Navy to fortify Guam. Representative Hamilton Fish of New York announced that fortifying Guam would be "a dagger at the throat of Japan." Congress turned down the Navy's request, and Guam would ultimately become defenseless.

Fortunately, even before World War I, our War Department and Naval Intelligence had serious misgivings about Japan's intentions and instituted a top-secret portfolio, christened WPO (War Plan Orange). Orange referred to Japan. The secret WPO essentially was to develop plans for any operation or anticipated action against Japan.

Even though Japan was a signatory to the Kellogg-Briand Pact in 1925, in which all the signatories agreed to outlaw war, Japan in 1931 launched an invasion of Manchuria. In response, the League of Nations issued a stinging condemnation. This resulted in the Japanese delegation unceremoniously walking out of the League's proceedings.

Never one to be held by any moral constraints in any of its agreements, Japan invaded China in 1937 and even attacked the U.S. gunboat *Panay* on the Yangtze River, sinking it with several of our men being killed or wounded.

The United States took a dim view in 1940 when Japan signed the Tripartite Pact with Hitler and Mussolini. By then Japan had occupied most of China's East Coast, along with large areas of Indo-China. In military parlance, Japan had already outflanked the Philippine Islands by its China and Indo-China occupations. The Tripartite Pact with its Axis partners guaranteed that should any of the three signatories be attacked by any other nation, and especially the United States, each would come to the other's assistance.

The United States called on Japan to halt its reckless excesses on the Asian mainland. In early 1941 the United States placed an oil embargo against Japan, along with freezing Japan's assets. The United States demanded that Japan withdraw from the Tripartite Pact as a quid pro quo for resuming trade. The United States also demanded that Japan pull its forces out of China and Indo-China and end its expansionist policy.

Finally, negotiations came to an impasse. A week before Pearl Harbor, an intercept picked up by our decoders, from Tokyo to Berlin, told the Japanese ambassador to tell Hitler and Ribbentrop that hostilities against the United States might come quickly by a clash of arms. On December 1, 1941, at a conference in Tokyo, the decision to go to war with the United States was made by the Japanese high command.

It would seem surprising that America's armed forces should be caught so unprepared at Pearl Harbor and in the Philippines when our State Department was armed with this vital information and with other information given to us by British intelligence of Japan's intentions. In the final analysis, however, all our prewar isolationists who would not stand up to Japanese expansionist aggression back in the 1930s finally had to eat crow.

About the Author

Joseph Friedman was born in 1923 in Brooklyn, New York. He proudly served his country as a combat marine with the Fleet Marine Force during World War II in three major South Pacific campaigns over a span of twenty-seven months. He currently lives in South Florida.

CPSIA information can be obtained
at www.ICGtesting.com
Printed in the USA
FSOW01n1020151216
28613FS

9 781450 232623